AF366819

Gerardo D'Orrico was born in Cosenza on March 6, 1976. After completing my high school, I attended the universities of Arcavacata (CS) and Bologna but without a degree, I have a good knowledge of computer science and some musical instruments. My youth was between the residence of Luzzi (CS) and Cosenza for studies or in the hometown of my mother Villapiana (CS) by the sea. I have made many trips in Italy and someone abroad, after the military service I helped my father with his work and I dedicated myself to writing prose as well as continuing my passion for computer science and software programming, I created and manage a web-site (beneinst.it) where everyone can enter their pages for free: letters, poems, drawings, pictures, photos. So far, I have published four books: 1. The good and the bad, memories 2. An ash ceiling 3. We Are Already Ten Minutes Ago 4. Say it yourself. I live in Luzzi where, among other occupations, I continue to write or revise my texts and research for technological art.

Original cover photo, GD 1986

Gerardo D'Orrico

An Ash Ceiling

Diary

Preface

This book is the second handbook-an account of contemporary life and personal diary written by me. The real joy that our time gives back through experiences, not a rediscovery of new technologies but a function in different historical and geological periods, what has already created it according to explanations of events and their solutions. A walk in the light of the Sun of the facts and enchantments, sometimes never revealed, perhaps too new and unusual, in a community that already has long been in need, as a wider and more slender voice, a tool to better insist on the day, really is not in a dream. Diary written in a simple way for a textual artistic form to justify even an initial and uncultured experience today. In style James Joyce's Ulysses is a book of good as a form of life, of art of the present, fundamental to exist free, alive is for sure. The period of the sixteen letters contained reaches from April 2007 to October 2008, english translation by Fatima Immacolata Pretta. Enjoy the reading,

Gerardo D'Orrico

1.
Mix & two

28.04.2007

Never lose your pen or your patience, never accept an evil in the house, it's never over, when it seems to be over it's not over, you need the right people, even when they all disappear, there's always someone left, it's when there's no one left, it's us. It happens at a time that is not part of the clock to exist, during what are called the day or night. The world has not fallen into a state of unconsciousness, on the contrary it has never been a day like this, this would not be a problem. Perhaps there are too many people but, in truth, there is no basic law for human structures already established in the year zero seven. So many thieves, so many planes to fly and to want on the planet. No problem in the eyes of a clear crystalline light, no uncertainty in the back of the car, no distortion of sound. The law is ours, life is not a centrifuge. One goes up in denial of an evil, as one can say that it does not exist, one must organize oneself for infinity which, however, one cannot remain here without it. The others have nothing to do with us, they are only images and yet they change us, the question arises, as I said to myself many years ago, what trouble it is to remove them from the image, what they have resulted in. You fight an evil since the death of Jesus, but, I'm still studying what they do to us in this century, maybe that's why time could be, a deception that hides the paradise, those who take care not to let anyone go there, as an absurdity is to reverse evil with good, an evil is a still life, while other people of rubber.

Allegories are not much digested by the national business software but, I assure you, they are a primary key to understand where to put your feet forward, it is difficult to understand, even simple things are impossible. My face is not mine, that if they will just want freedom of expression, what we will give if not the envelope of what we are, all 'the true or false that we do not know, nothing stops but, there are rules you do not stay apart, with the deception that you do not exist. It remains a photocopy of what it was, it is insistently you want to be, what is life then seems to me to be peace or, a starting point towards what they will never let us live, to free myself I don't even know what I did, I remember a series of positive and negative things.

Free all evil and you'll see you'll be alone, they told me it had arrived, but then I saw who he was associated with, that is to think about that abyss, the world is unfair. Run, run then you get tired, shoot then the ammunition runs out but, a game has already started, we are inside, we just have to follow the arrows, whoever sees us is only God for the moment, he doesn't stop, if you don't stop. Try to stop and you get shot but, you can't run away forever, there are those who ran away forever but, it's not really the way of those who have to die on the ground. The opposite of an ideal plan is a normal day, the everyday. A breath of fresh air, as it is dear here in Italy to breathe we pay, we give emotions of love or other works, which are what it should be, every moment continuous.

A good may seem an exaggeration of what it is, always being happy, when you are in love, drunk or paid not an invention. I don't normally curse, I don't offend and, I don't transgress what is good, there are people who advise us to do it, then it is logical that one feels bad, with all those problems, those screams in the house of people who contravene each other, without even knowing why kill a false good, more than the others. They are suicidal their idols, their leaders, perhaps slave souls of some afterlife is they worship there, they will be slaves of hell too, or, they could never have any idea what hell is, so they want to see. A good thing is to go beyond hell, to look at what you see, then the word is not enough, you have to go deeper but, in reality you have already just passed it, you are already free of the space around you. You have to respect yourself first and last but, you remain as if you were just born, you don't know how to do it. Time forms what is right, the first trace of the visual and sound direction of our being. The first thing to do is not to offend ourselves, then the ten commandments, a surprise is to find God at the end of the road, one who wants to kill us.

A big mistake is believing that an evil could be a good, an evil is an evil, wants the evil, the same good for the good stop, instead I hear people every day who want to discuss this. Certainly, it is a mathematical resolution between what counts and what we have left but, the after is everything, like saying the total is not even because even afterwards. The dysfunction distributed even today cannot be recovered tonight, without the use of external agents, you cannot be zombies all day, then in the evening free us to commit suicide. Yesterday I saw a good evil, today I have very much present the enemy they have already drawn, what ruins lives to steal its essence. A good has never stolen anything, it's an explanation of what you wear, it's inside you find yourself; I think it's the suit after the end of the world, paradise. An evil is right in front of us, all day long, making us become a beautiful zombie, a human without movement, both physical and mental, at most an individual freedom, it's a copy of a good, it should be the good today. Here we are in Italy, it starts in the north and ends in the south, the whole territory is with the same laws, property and freedom of opinion. Lack in summary of evil is a mistake that we pay daily, to the relationship with others, it is always good that solves everything, burn them, there are only a few blunders left in this hell of forgotten where they have closed us.

Since the environments there want to decide the others, an obscurity as it is written, makes us forget to go beyond what others live. It seems to me that the human environments where we live are not registered at all in Italian law, at the same time I see almost nothing and no one who does. Illegal as if it were nothing, it is then a public work to level the light has always been the work of someone, they themselves boast of who knows what they have done, others there praise. I think nowadays, small political, bureaucratic or legal manoeuvres would create a stable system, without the manual help of man, instead there are those who want more blood, people who sacrifice their lives to support the weight of a society that is not, does not want to do anything, that has to die according to astral calendars. Dreaming of a better world, is to die every day for everyone, the deception is already discovered, the future is already a fact, will be moved this forest to see again, to see a man, thank you.

Today I am traveling for a holiday very close to my family, at the sanctuary of Santa Maria of arms in Cerchiara of Calabria. An evil is not good, like other misfortunes of these times, wretched is our life, destined to follow, in the very good sense we will be avenged by the future. Beatings you know, they stop people who can't stand them, they are tired or, they have no more arguments to explain their super-arrival on the planet. I'm a bit drunk as a consequence from misfortune to misfortune, the good only happens in the light, because it's a shine but, no matter who has chosen for me, for you, for everyone, has already passed.

Loneliness is a rare gift, a precious moment, what you pay to be alone. I try to understand why the hands of a clock erase the memory, I smoke a cigarette and I don't know whether to forget you or, in order to preserve you, to resist to find you again.

Kisses, G

2.
Obero, the act of oppressing

28.07.2007

"To get out of a trap…"

Strikes to render us unconscious of the day that is coming, in broad daylight or in the evening, to understand how to strike others or, to personify ourselves, to take away our identity. At the same time, I realized that if I or someone else presents or acts for the good, it cannot remain in an immobile position. In the meantime, I find the day confusing, without goals, since they have been cancelled since the beginning of the day, I think it was done to everyone I know, involved in having to do the things that had to be done. Events that are handed down waiting for the end of time, also because as I already know, a good has prerogatives, we will have to do even those things that have taken away from us, they bothered him and had to be done, like the environment of the village, even shrivelled up citizen, cancelled in the forces of those who do not know that only move forward and backward a human being. Hardly as obvious, we will certainly get out of this situation or trouble, we simply cannot continue indefinitely, because we are not a corporal infinite, but the fact that when everything breaks we rebuild it, to function again as if nothing had happened, I always hope in your clemency and your benevolence, the last words of those who momentarily rejoice in this reality, as a bottle has already ended. Time grows, yes of course, every act is not wrong, as it is part of a life, but there are tangibly acts that hurt in its course, certainly but not, drinking bleach. Of course, they want to kill us, even so to say or to do, people cannot see moving objects, especially the head, do not want to hurt me but, I always carry it with me, because I live in the day, today the modern.

Those problems are personal, not sick people, there is no need moment by moment to go and see if an evil is really an evil, the same good, then instead it is a right to privacy or a robbery, so on and so on five minutes in the morning, you already understand that it is not really to do what they say, how they say it, what they promised us or, they will make us do. It will kill you for sure, but only if you always stay still, no more, in short, in reality time itself takes away those things that you can't do, it's as if someone remembers you, you will always die one day, while you will always remain beautiful and alive. Rest assured you're alive, it's a very important fact for the large number of people present, how can you not like to go out and find the next ones talking? you know that 'time washes everything. An asocial after five years changes personality, it becomes very social, friendly, this is what modern society does. Who makes these tests of good, has as murder existential fame, as it is not very clear for some causes you die is nobody admits it, one could be the assumption of evil.

So you study your time bomb, so that you are not in that place when it explodes, then you invent a bar where you can remain indifferent or, do something you like, then you go on in your city to get to lunch, dinner, then the blue. You have to move, even if we inevitably fall back into us because, you can't always start over. Better to die was said in Italy, then after all death was after two hours, it was not at all a happiness but, what I personally did not do anything, is to pretend not to die. Keep living, do nothing, just die, so don't believe in this not very colourful environment, a bad thing here is money. You only believe in our yes, writing we are not very interested in evil, the important thing is that we have not been given, they cannot come to tell us in ten years that we are pigeons, if we are studying something else. The body weight is not only water, you'll see that we don't go down to earth anymore, since I never go down either, I've never gone down into evil, so quiet your soul, talking about quieter of the false. This front is just a business tool, later opens in fantasy, otherwise there is no opposite to a single or a reason that doubles life, does not continue tonight life? No leverage, no grip, no harm, from me think of the future. A guy lives, eats the banquet has nothing to do with it, more than anything else you have never called any of the people who are just an idea, laughs without being a fool, is not who goes crazy with evil or, who has never had a future. Someone will come and stop you, a neighbour or two, tell you to stop doing what you're doing. If you don't understand the present, think of the future.

Ok we don't do anything anymore, let's relax in our evening or, the evening is no longer ours but of them who don't know, it will seem strange to you or maybe you already know, they are happy to die, we don't, we don't make any difference. Ok then it doesn't go, it's already gone, or it will happen ok, then it's not there, and yet another thing is coming, however, live communism if there are still communists, living together is to separate from fascism in life, a parasite leans to the right. What manages not to make us talk, if the solution is beings, thinks that others are also beings, is eating well but healthy. Enter your well-being is not to think about erasing houses, when the past is a past, the present always smells good.

So it does not go, so you do not know, so who wants, after the interests will not be theirs but ours. We rest without participants, without love like blackberries, aim at the center ... they want to see us in a bar to drink a coffee or, in the house then go out like Methuselah when it comes out of the bath, you are fine. Maybe there isn't, he doesn't breathe the deception of a world incapable of making two feet and the interest between us. I am white, yellow, the colour of water for an evil overcome, green because I still love you. An evil is not a friend but, a dull form that reassures people, so that nothing has happened but, later perhaps it will attack us, because the future is fulfilled. There is no control, the past is a window to the future, the world does not see it, we never say its presence, because it is the false, it is a nightmare.

So today not everything is good, not everything has entered... don't say I told you so, the poison is like that, life is not eternal, how will you be able to go home without an angel, without eating and sleeping, without even understanding why you have been alive. We haven't all been there together but, one by one, don't hide the good Mr. Nobody, alive is let live. How many ways there are to die in these badly created ideas, only one to live, they never told us, these big modern heads, so continues even today, even if it seems a diminutive or an increased, that's how we live alone, or rather we continue in the impossibility of looking for a decent equation or, a Cartesian product that produces us, instead of an emotion other than love or, then an accomplice for evil. Maybe it's late so we don't have to complain, because it's already too much what we have, too much really, an exaggeration let's see... that product to eat in the kitchen says something, then the usual up and down the stairs, trying not to meet someone but, it's impossible, maybe we would have made the wrong year, you know they do it to everyone that use.

Whoever I made the mistake will leave him in the wrong, what he thinks he's making a basket, a hole. Here really there are only beautiful packaged products, only to use for a long time, so to say new, is then you cannot increase. What was doing a bad thing is not a basket but, only all the diseases put together in the vacuum or, what makes you lose the good from what I understood, a grown-up being who grows up is does not understand if not sometimes, if they then find that you have understood, they attack you so, until the pizzas and cakes are not finished, they are if not deserts, small things like all diseases, good appetite.

Bye, G.

3.
The song of the future

14.09.2007

"What you have to do, it's called the future."

To understand a good you need to be enrolled friend, but from this you need to be alive, that is, awake not asleep, then the sequel. Sometimes I am surprised to find myself in the future that is today, looking at the technology that I find myself, thinking the future really comes. What you're fighting for sure you win, a first problem is always to be able to stay there too, bodily to see it. Everything is over, so begins the theory of a better life, packable, consumable, because we are finished and completed drawings, theories that impress our day. Primitive drawings that gave the beginning, are the trace of a door to the future, a door that eliminates time, that opens the mind to an instant, without the perception of pain or feeling.

A good thing really happens, the image of our dream comes true. Without time, history opens up, without envy or evils of any kind. Find a common language or create a software, the basis of a speech is built in more or less human realities, in the memory of having had ancestors. Art is not suffering but, a part of liberation, because after suffering, I never liked the discomfort, no dilemma in general, to begin with the complications are a disaster, we have done what was necessary at least once a day, if then by habit you organize yourself is alive in the year zero seven, you can trust invest, do not fool yourself with those ideas, it is true that they liberate.

When the water will be finished I will take leave of absence, we do not suffer at all cumulative, we do not lack anything, it is just a blasphemous illusion of the world, you have done everything trustworthy, there is not twice as much nothingness in a human unit, at most it will be a small abrasion, then only fantasy or depression, there are no people not compensated for the day, to think about it well will be a person or, an object close to us that understands what we lack, they want to take away our future, the future, what we will do, is just another way to make us die in their place. How many wars, then peace does not exist, you have a stopwatch to understand since when what will not be or, is never. Problems are death lines, not having is still death, words that cannot be used, are the death of thought. Places where they make us stay is you can't say it, because nobody will believe it anyway, a classic. You suddenly see who is evil, where no one can say they have been, there are no places where you have been that you cannot say.

Is the end the beginning?
Bye, G.

4.
Arachnophobia

20.11.2007

"The meeting's not happening, is it? There are forces that condition our main interest, the non-existence can be a denunciation of evil. The social sometimes, people confused with objects."

The exit doesn't exist... it's a key to solve our problems, to do only an inner study to find an exit. Together everything is more beautiful, to be is to think, say, do, kiss or die. When we are no longer there, don't look at us but at the part that was there. Power has always been a body, the mind a builder, now you don't know where it is going to lead, a fulfilment. Remaining in the good is the contact with all the things you have, a continuous flow of people in birth, makes us reborn in life, others live because you are a past, an adult, what you see is what you have produced.

The state is the good that wasn't there, what proceeds must be better than the things that don't work. The basis of human non-thinking is evil, the speech must be made away from the eyes and head, from a book or a sheet of notes, do not get confused about the position, even in the kitchen to bake means the elimination. We are goods of the world from that we are all in the world, an evil is a waste of time.

To go against good is to feel bad in person, a basic confusion. Continuing one must move-re, like if y moves from x infinitely, it happens that the equation is unsolvable. Communism is a dream, we are not all the same, so the state hasn't yet arrived at work or, an evil continues and it's all real, isn't it? the state is an incoming good, then you over-come it but, whenever it was.

Here nothing is true, overcome to breathe is an-other reason, so if y is not x, another world can be reversed in concrete, then the rest is all a real fake, there is no imagination, there are people who 'the problem really have it.

Respect doesn't know what it is, don't even tell them, there would be no need. So the air has been cut into slices, there is almost nothing left, a question full of other people's problems, it is difficult to think about the reality of others.

The cobweb is the taste of not being there, evil understands yes, everything is already ready what is needed, and what is not needed, what a bad world is ahead of us, the life that normally goes on, from today vote Craxi, where there is not, there will not be, *G.*

5.
Remain unparalleled

22.12.2007

"What is possible in a world where coherence no longer exists, the body is the habitat of how you are. Where we come from, where we are, not from shortcomings we will understand what we need, but in reason."

What we have been is already enough to live and to laugh, as 'the future is the most beautiful fruit that life can give us. The air is tasted, the tastes and voices of people are new things that light up the senses, to the good fortune of meeting again or, if we have never seen each other, without the danger of falling is not to see anymore. Power is life, without rancour. I liked to abandon perdition for the belief, that false light and that rotting stench for life, the perfume, the smell. The memory of being finished, as it was before for the celebration of what it is today. Surprising me that the future exists, seeing everything reassessed, even myself. To live happily an accomplished tomorrow, the fresh and paid air, a slight burn in the brain that allows us to breathe, without the memory of those people who fly and talk badly. Free not to be there, living is not believing in the unhealthy fantasies of the whole world. People can be medicines or even sicknesses, the internet of humans is the truth that builds us, never throw away what you have earned with experience, it always serves. What we could do is only us, existence is like an object. To believe is existence, who believes exists. A small flight of bones, of flesh, of spirit, towards an intellectual security that takes the fruit of a healed body, because of him. Breathing the reality of a single thought, it is then difficult to make it concrete, as we were in the beginning, then a persistent catastrophe that does not go away, a stain that can no longer go away, we are all born, who arrives is lost.

Salvation dwells high up, my head turns sometimes, it will be the emptiness but, try to engage in a speech not turned off, try to taste another coffee, our speeches have always been lit, unleashed.

Today is not a day like any other, today is more than tomorrow but there are those who think that all the words are wrong or the presence, the heat, the two of us, all of us or just me. Who knows what has changed people's memory, where the common thought of communicating so as not to always say the same words has gone, you will certainly find it at home, all crumpled up somewhere, along with real imagination. There is a reason for all the works or thoughts, for how many of us is not normally consistent with today's act, only the good exists but, to be so it is difficult to start from now stop, another you yourself ... not only complaint and persecution, as it was in the year zero seven, I think it will be the same even now where you are. Wounds that have long tormented in the distant planet Earth, have even now the visa and sighed what it is to communicate not to speak, not to write not to fill in.

There are things that you cannot do is are beautiful in their form or, others that have formed modern life, from these you can understand your own historical period, if you want in relation to the human figure, social even yourself. A strange but good theory for good, it says goes better and better and better. It's a law of the body where we went to breathe better, then better what will be, you study on purpose to understand better or, what is said for better. Of the movements of the body we cannot there to understand each other or, we lack the breath ... we are not yet finished, not deciphered. It will also be true that we don't have to admit the presence of evil or other questionnaires that we will never complete, because they have been taken away to make others do them, others that won't be needed.

Logic and time are coherences, or necessarily you are without a part, there is no part, there is no part, we do not exist for the moment or, better to say, this moment does not exist. In the meantime we are here, even if we succeed without extinguishing ourselves, I remind you that to extinguish from here is to die, not to go. Who is a fake does evil, is certainly an inferior to those who suffer it, who does evil is an evil almost always, the law does not protect him, okay. We are not party favours or, dizzying falls down, we are unmade phone calls.

The world works with gasoline, how well you do good, how with the law you will feel a thousand times better, the law is all forever, it will become a necessity to remain consistent, laugh ah! ah! Just a touch to breathe, no bats, a flight of what remains, a legal act to denounce, the rest is you. So many things to do now... there's no strength left! Ease in the flow of blood into the body, it is said the presence or, the absence of a cut as fantasy or, I play other world.

You have to overcome the normal rules of understanding, art is not wrong but passed in the modern day or century in which I live. In the perseverance of not encountering the horrible sight of what you are not, what you live can also be the amount of things you say or don't say, only a darkness remains, what you expected no longer lives, only a lit flame guides our body to a new home, not to always laugh at what happened to us. Unknown the source of our private questions, it's a strange situation, living with problems that can't be solved, even stranger. Cruel is the Savior, where are you going far from my house? the intention was without verifying an act, there is always something to do ... look back, you can start from where you always want, without ever drawing compensation from what you are not.

I've seen all the theoretical forms that can't take a real form and, of the real forms that don't have a theory, death never happens, you don't leave, you don't erase anything, maybe it's just past but, however it exists, it's a duty to remember, indeed it's to go where you can, and avoid the rest that you don't have to. The others are all fake, it's just that it's not really, so you insinuate that you already know it, photocopies of things that you didn't have to bring, for the rest you could see. The world is lost, the big words are false, I advise you to be alone, don't use false equals, it's alive. What we call the emptiness you can find instead in the company, who never or well use the equals, is the same crippled, as it is a false good, deep down the reality is, like the city at night, does not accept fakes. What will they do again, to get us used to doing evil! Who knows what they will say even before they stop forever, for the whole world you always have to do a lot of math, before going home, so always the turn one, two, three times.

Out of a world, more than wounded wet, good to go out, pity that there is no one outside the houses except the few. You see it's raining, it's still there are things-businesses that can't be decided, facts of the matter speak of others in your house, they do it in everyone's house! Well, it should be better, rest later, you don't know how many things to learn in school is later, not even a thing. In my opinion these lessons are the future, they live together with us or, otherwise, people who take advantage of them. We will not exist in anything, just the air that enters our bodies, nice and true but, believe me offended and prejudiced for this is too much, fresh air maybe. Betrayed lives are the best thing to enter, where the mediocrity of the lowest people does not enter, a game to get rid of at a certain age, but hurry up and that's all it was. Freed from the game of parts, that's what you live by false fascism. You feel better if you say it's not true but, to hear it is one thing to talk about it is another, other things are all another matter.

The verb is all things, every law and religion. Sometimes it can always be better to talk about other things: the end of a day, the end of a year, things you don't say, things already said. A stalemate to be reorganized, a situation that will surely come to an end.

Happy holidays. Gerardo

6.
What is good is not exceeded

30.01.2008

"Of still images and asterisks that don't turn, don't trust."

From the mummification of everyday life you cannot leave without a breath of air, the same living without the dissolution of belief, you cannot exist without power, is to think that the air and art, are or are not the same thing, for many but, not always the dismissal of the Government is peace without failures or surprises. What remains from the envy suffered by other few but believing people, is not only sleep, but also the belief of an ungrown popular consciousness, as water may seem oil. From where you are, do not give up, do not compromise, the best of opportunities is offered without even thinking that you can have to give, without ever meeting again.

Where we are not, we won't be the modern tends to make the future a known thing, the best way for me is to think that tomorrow will be different from today but, together with today, what God has reasoned is undoubtedly right but in short not a mass suicide, as those evils advise now uh, they will always do it safe. Basically false that personally present themselves, rumours that are not a neighbourhood, where not staying costs life but only a wrong place, as there are still places where you always go is never win God, the Moon, the Sun, more not to win when you die.

It seems to me that 'the bottom is just another fall back of a larger bottom even the false one, then as I turn my head is I see that I am already at the end of the line, because we had yet to arrive, what we expected, we are not or the State what? Of our brain what is left in a sea of ideas that do not exist, without a common thought that for them is a mistake. We pretend we don't know it, they'll even reset us false, of course! In this sea it's not but, a lake springing from a labyrinth of things that I don't build good but bad ideas, prerogatives from buildings where you can't always be there but, just go and see if in that other place that doesn't exist, you're not exploited.

People at night become bottles of bitter essences, it is secretly you continue, you must understand that you cannot leave, not to lose, you must have the ability to understand, is not to exist in nothingness, in emptiness. Thinking can be improved in the moment when the things that exist are a fundamental help to establish themselves in the future, as unique people. Rarely can one encounter what is said or, one has the possibility of not understanding the void as the solution is in time. The next action is a clear sign that identifies the past for you too, so creating a chain of days, months is to realize who you are talking about and, see other details in the way you want, as where it is to end, the error that does not make us come up from a good grave well. In the bureaucracy of language, of expression, fear will stop to dissolve unspoken things, which serve to create the future.

It's an interchangeable society, take what they gave or did to you and say goodbye to them, everything is in order just because they didn't kill you. Go on living, experiences are life really here, I warn you an equal: don't talk about good and evil, it makes you fall out that you are no longer you. I'm always looking for a software installed or to be installed, certainly there is no certificate in this stadium uh, State, if you are not there, where you go to appear, where you are no longer left. Gifts will come, thank you, I knew it, in fact they'll let you know about the car. Good morning maybe boredom is already a pretext, not to talk anymore? or the evidence crushes a temporary evil, what really could not be. You may not live, but there is light, happy.

I have noticed when everything is still in peace, that moment could be able to transform itself, normality transfigured without legal registrations, my face changing without something more that seemed to me before, a way of life does not exist or, it is a fact of ours to observe people well. The need to quarrel with me does not exist at all, for everything its place but, as you see, peace is not spoken about, the order for which it was requested will be done, no peace we change the subject, where dreams go, the important thing for them is to stay somewhere. Without having the idea of what it is then, being is not seeing, as in that day we were not more than what we remembered, but what happens to us, not only happens to ourselves yes, I know I'm annoyed to always talk about the usual things but, what you want a life without you or without a goal.

There is a wonderful evening that promises nothing, we will expect in a world without evil, I cannot even tell you try not to kill you, we are in an uncomfortable position but, it is the best we can have now, I'll tell you where we went for the holidays but do not delude yourself, it was just a break, just cannot believe in anything, from this the meaning of where they have done the evil // // that denouncing, speaking is the same, it is not the State in the eyes of many, it seems an exaggeration but it is a problem, it already exists for some time, as a mistake not to worry about it, it is only the evil that wanted to make itself beautiful, even today then, the fact is already past, a deception arises from which to leave, because we are so distracted by our years.

Too many things ahead, the technology we hoped for is you continue to dream, then you grow along with retro progress. Tomorrow is not an end or, other pacts for outdated people, what are outdated people? Good is good for everyone, people are not toys, everything else was as wrong as what we are living. Everything can't be said or, one can't bear to say that evil exists. Here we end up starting somewhere else, but somewhere we should arrive, like spaceships arrive on the planet or, like people released from extra-terrestrials.

Two palm trees, the birds, the sea and the sun, one day in the afternoon, which was not the same thing. Too many walls between people, you say more than walls, will be other things. If you don't see any difference between good and evil, in the end they have already eliminated you or, you want to be avenged, depending on whether it never happened. So what is the future in this century, a known thing, is this the new thing? The return from where you want, it has not been organized but, on the other hand, it is happening today, what the past expected.

A software is what solved today, virtual reality will grow, believe me many other projects have hidden, not to let us know the culture, the law, the bureaucratic, they thought or wanted us to think that it was a game, especially the point where we were not betrayed or, they betrayed us but, we betrayed ourselves. Nothing worrying yes, just that they make it pass for the only good, as they move tracks that move our lives to the wrong places or, a portable avalanche from which you have to move, in addition they create what you have to do, sometimes even forbidden.

Time washes its stains, with the rain and, in good weather, tries to leave those problems away, don't pay as much attention to them, as when you finish a job you are happy with the past. Now they pay you the future comes is also what you expected, it's not a joke, it's a fantasy, it's our father's evil that you are heaven free us from them, ok how to live yesterday or in the past is a visual art but, if you are today, it's later, while the non-existence has always been a question that every society has had to explain itself, to put out words for exercise, is not just a legal form, a practice that does not belong to you or, you don't have to do it, as some precious are crystals of educational castes, as reality is for everyone, as other subjects serve to remain speechless, recover what has never been possible, that is today.

People want to play? you do not understand a question mark. In a stormy sea, where is the quiet? Where there is no more wind in the sea. A good was not a private thing or, a crystal to eat, to drink, to understand and distribute or, other public issues that we hope will be resolved, closed in their empire of the municipality, there are no doubts, we will not remain finished and/or failed would be like saying, nothing has happened instead everything has happened. Arriving where others do not land was a success, getting lost to not see that themselves, was a game that at a certain age you lose. Believing that there is no longer a future, where believing is like arriving in a city, it is not tomorrow but what can happen with a little more well-being, without having the problems that yesterday is perhaps today's life. Submerged by very large questions that are actually giant words, used for purposes are not complacent to use. The trick is to keep the big words always considered as important, the rest you can see in a package that you find in your trusted store.

What's the problem? Here it's all joy or death then, life is always the same, one only has to manifest oneself in good and established things everywhere. What will the future be made of? being a mortal for sure death, then you try to think about something else, the why of time passing. In reality we are already built, we are already born, what happens is us more what we do, perhaps it is forbidden not to know how difficult everything is already, that is, drunk. I'm tired at home I just turned off the ship, I'm almost decided as usual in a few hours to go to sleep. We need a decisive solution in the day, a fixed point on which to base tomorrow with all the rules that will involve but, many will have already understood, what I wanted to say.

That road is too long, you don't have to follow it, you don't know where it goes. Everything goes where it is appropriate, without making many problems then in the end it turns off, it ends up being complete. Study the positions is how come there is no afterwards, only if you say it you make a mistake. The world changes, all the things you don't say, what seems like a huge issue, then it's us.

The Earth shines like a star, doing good today is like carrying a stigmata... may life always smile on you, and the Sun in your heart never dies, the road is always long but at the end there is the arrival, *G.*

7.
Leaving fascism forever

29.02.2008

"I'm just saying, it's not the same thing as stating the truth."

It seemed like it was over, but it was another day, any other day, even today, you don't know, you can't know. It will be just another way of saying it, also because today is the decisive day, you have to make yourself strong, or other continuous breakthroughs of a discourse where we no longer exist. You remain as the bottle of what you have not drunk, drenched in what you have never been, gagged in front of a future that we do not know, you cannot afford the past for which 'the forbidden. Basically they want to command us without understanding what exists in front of us, without conscience. What you haven't asked for, they won't give it to you, we'll have to go and see what we don't have, don't sleep if possible... don't betray yourself when they tell you to cheat the other, which one they didn't tell us, they told us it was wrong, then they'll solve that we all do good, they don't see that what some people say can't even be repeated.

And here are our buildings that we could no longer see, given today we are surprised, because tomorrow we could not get there, because no one can speak, it's all wrong or, what you don't have you can't see, what obtuseness in objects and related things, the law is only one then, it's true from which you cannot dissociate yourself, the road we walk seems the path of a lifetime, the years are always growing but, who has understood doesn't know anything, between us I say why? Obviously we needed to talk about everything but, where you find a prohibition think about it then cross it, it was just the useless there was nothing to do, we spent a day in the afternoon.

I bought an Italian CD tonight I'm going to eat pizza, time goes horizontally but, it's true that tomorrow I'll have to work, I won't be very rich. When the words end, a speech doesn't end but, not even begin from what I see or what should or could be today, there's still a lot to set up but many still don't know what exists today, in the present or, why someone doesn't have.

Where does that road lead that never ends, that never finds the real end? Here is that road that leads nowhere ends, you don't get there. It's better to change it with an easy one, take the one to go back home, the one you know, you'll see they'll tell you that you've made a mistake but, what do you want to care about it, the important thing is that you get there, there's no better place than the one you already know, maybe it leads to self-destruction leave it alone, we're not all immortals or evils. What has already been done is done, as it has already been solved helps, while what we don't know can't govern us but can scare us. What we do not accept now is the same as always, false fascism in the contemporary, life as an admission of elimination or staying locked in a box, so then you have to choose the original objects, to have their true function, but you also need to see what you initially wanted ... careful many sun damage.

In reality there is fascism is not over but, later on they will take it away, stay to look at this strange world that needs eyes to see and people who work, we live where a description is a nothing, a blank page of a white painting, in fact they kill us just because we occupy a place. A rebirth is a flower that is born every morning, a single unknown, instead of problems can be born many. The heart is like a strawberry, if you don't lose, you don't live.

The time of day is music can be divided into bars, four quarters or more complex, problems like flowers, can be detected and understood, where the explanations are no longer there, you are at the starting point, again do not think about it, and it is always the usual problem what is not you, there is no reason not to believe that it is no longer you, but another to live for you. They are problems that want explanations, not to be problems anymore, not perfect creators who declare themselves free men. Explanations that no one has given us, to which we should give a sense to continue, are thought to win people who have already lost, as certain positions that the daylight must clean to see them.

The day only illuminates what remains of us, they want to steal our dear conscience without difference or distrust. When we finish talking about ordinary people, to talk about objects anyway... if one takes away the war from you, he thinks that he no longer loves you, and what's more, they bring us bodily extinction like nothing will be the salad, who knows perhaps there is no sense in modern society, the consciousness of not believing that we are alone, but even there they bring us evil. To carry an evil then it is fashionable, it is right not to know, better locked up in jail instead of opening our eyes, even if it means broadening our conscience, our memory or the police station.

Something in the food is not good but, I confess everything is good, left a bad is what it would be, the unknowns that you cannot know by staying in line, a geopolitical position in our house or, in the park where it suits us. The geometry of presence is very important, we are always. Who didn't think he was capable? It must have been a flaw in the hood, we can all understand a whole good, of course. This is society, there are no others, here it is created, wherever you want, you can exist. We are not here, it's not safe to feel better there, we need more laws, less banging and time, all the realities we can understand if understanding is to follow but, above all, to want our own part. There is a time for all things, well you see that there had to be, you cannot become just ornaments and decorations of the city, at a certain time the state of the regime of sub-contracting, you cannot stand it anymore, are uninstalled speeches our thoughts, our ideas are already part of the modern judiciary, is then what is not held is not part of real life, as what the state has not yet hurried. At the end of the day we should become a state that expels the state, what is not clear, it is still an evil, a current question, the old problem, when it will appear will be good laughs, not knowing what to do or, not knowing what it is. Who wants to command then will be defined uh, annihilated, what we complain if the weight is always specific, legal acts that everyone lives in the future will be described or, arrested in a police blitz, always.

History has never seen worse moments than those that are told to live today, everything is unreliable, incredibly false and approved, there is no way out of the destruction that has come, they are all stronger than you, than me who are the only ones to die, day by day without any real friend who can help us, laugh. All ruined and ruining, no way out, it would be too much, it would be better to get out of this prison but by now we are stopped, we have been stopped in our small space, where we have sinned, our sin is our source of normality and, other things-idiocies that I am not here to list you, also because maybe I am tired. Things of grownups, perhaps even too much, or dull as they declare the fact finished or, the act too great that no one can perform. Truth that is clear at least that one, you had glimpsed what it was before, then no one should dare to think that reason has no way to fill itself. Easy realities it is useless to go on to death, trivial things are essential, to believe in ourselves, your source is one, the others belong to others, you must take your then, go on to what verbs can give you. Calm down, nothing happens, not even one speaks because he doesn't hear, what you can do or don't do, if you don't want to breathe anymore, like you there are others, we will all breathe tomorrow, this will be enough. Law is a continuous bio system towards a good, look what kind of friends we are, it says how you dare to speak. A fact that is absolutely always the same, we are the ones under discussion, nothing will happen for those issues, it is only the number of relationships that will change. The return is part of the departure, in a quarter of an hour you decide your normal day that, can be enhanced, then we will close perhaps you know.

Excuse me for breaking into your house again but, what are you doing the beginning of an evil? think if they could know about the existence of good, where you have gone to stop, what air they make us live, fascism is the greatest infamy that man has been able to consider lately, then think in the false one, even if only because those uncertain practices are already solved, where we should grow up, instead no one brings his affections with him. Everything is already resolved as Christ commands, look what exists on the other side of the window, how you are there or, you will never be there.

It's evening there's almost nothing left to do, just think that it couldn't be better, just retrieve all the files to put them in line. The work ennobles the man, you have to pay us, it was not true it all seemed false, instead it was just that thing resembling a human, which still passed by here, to take away the attention: it's a game of entrepreneurs take or leave, consider it's all done while you finish, as it's no longer worth doing anything else, you and everything is over.

Better leave the war here or, at home, I have on one side the green on the second floor, something exists believe me, the function was to have learned because you cannot know or, because it is too much but, in a form of education, you can not only know who wants to exploit you. Knowledge must be established as law, that person more than a fake in the end, it seemed to me a suicide. He wanted to be me then, in another time, he would say to me the things that I had to say to him, while I didn't have to say them to him before, because he said that they were wrong, it was for me to say them to him. Society grows and we will not be part of it, but what is being invented, society is what you have paid or, what they have stolen from you or, what you believe.

Now or later no one will ever know, but even in static form, still there is always a need for information or, associations are too ambitious. What virus you come from, what more than anything else will blind you or, they will kick you out. You won't be a being, you won't have a future all the time, you'll still have to look at that line or, that point that your fake friend stole from you to get attention. Today you don't respect anything but, a respect is a good that leads life, do you have something to buy that will give you value? Don't think about it, slowly moving towards your stasis, which is not that of an unhealthy person, who leans on your shoulders for a living.

Forget that it will be the business of others or, matters of an evil, of those who want to lead there and those who want there, who bring you there, but what will we know of what is an infection or, of things as dear as sicknesses. Uncompleted betrayals, think from how you make a change you can see the people around you or, the municipality, the rest of the things that are lost or, that have been wrong. What they teach you in school as a loser, understand who's busy is.

In that downstairs where you don't live, downstairs where you don't think there can be such a downstairs... was it even false? What don't you believe, don't you see, what matters is math is animal! We are living, we feed ourselves, we would have laws, we would die in a lower place than that, or we are in Fascism or, in the year one thousand nine hundred and fifty. It's another absurd thing that wins us, it solves what wouldn't happen if you left it alone. Maybe there is an evil in Italy, but what kind of equalized society is this, let's do it for good a good that is amplifying it, it's the same as they say, but it's not true, it's certainly an evolution of thought, then we'll see for a goal. We are already married to many things, don't you think. Normally what can anarchy, what is hidden? What they stole from us, what we won't have, what we want to know, we won't know. There is a wrong malicious thought and, a right thought what it was, begins with a concrete and coordinated movement of the arts. A real basis of good is a software or, a programming language. That of evil, on the other hand, annoyance. While you give a hand to yourself, give it to others.

Bye, G

8.
Dreams, time

31.03.2008

"Good will change the use, customs and language commonly used."

Are we alone in evil or, for better, there's nothing, we're a prison or good things. Presence is the most important act, but the game was upside down, what had happened is part of that cancer that Europe has been carrying for a long time. Ignorance is only a part in people, different if you want from what we could expect, who wants to steal the identity was an evil, it bothers them again, wanting to appear.

Existence is an alternative to what is the obvious, so it had to go let's just let the bosses say that, then they are also a part of our brain, as what we have associated with our favourite food. So many times life could give us something more, you've seen something new, just dreams or stay to get lost. You have to think something new, if new is a word that has a concrete meaning, it is not just realizing a dream, life is a dream. The rest of the sentence is superfluous, it only remains what is needed or, what is not yours. Other words can be contagious, who is not attached to the present, it is said that cleanliness is the best of the rules in this time, as 'the need for order is the basis of the human being. Better cannot be asked, if not knowing more from within, as belongings that today could always be better, if amplified with a voice, which is missing in many speeches. To know exactly the name of the contact with other people, even those not identified. Identity is fundamental or, other concepts that might seem fascist, in reality deal only with art or, in fact, the body of a human being that is an arm, eyes, head, hands and more, it is not true that there is no order but, that has been clouded by the minds of people already rendered unconscious, so the depth become obvious. Clear signs created by the lack of expressions of what we are to others, of what we cannot say, by the use of customs that declare themselves modern.

We do not exist, it is already the too much of those who justify our modern age, everything is bad or, nothing is bad. Flying against the wind is all we need, we must procure the whole world in a pocket, the remote past all as a resource. Nothing better, get out as soon as the weather clears up. New things that have to come, arrive, are not like people who miss appointments or trains. We will not change the Earth, she already thinks what we will transform and, as she must change us, we must also adapt to build our speech of revolution, then times have changed was normal. Another day is said to reassure the elderly before dying, in this world that is perhaps mine, they make us live without recording what more there could be, because it is forbidden to always use those damn words, dreams are freedom and life.

Calmness is the secret of all things, in free spaces you find a solution to your penance, it is not true that another concrete one is without escape route, there is a way to record reality, even if you can't get out. We cannot change the world is who changes us, it must be one of those speeches, what seemed to be instead is now, as is the boredom that gives us the way not to stay among those in the zoo. Tomorrow is another day, a fruit of today. What you do today will be tomorrow but, it's a struggle to stand, you spend what time has given us for good, without looking at what is necessary. Justifications are useless, what you are is what you have done, don't you believe in a speech that frees us or in those who imprison us instead? The solution is here with those who understand and those who don't know, there are no people who don't understand or can't understand. A fixed point does not understand, move it to the forefront is not you. The speeches are not always the same, certainly one positive and one negative, after all you will see the time alone washes the mistakes there is written, believe me people get big and sometimes they end ... memories of having already met everyone today and, the damn time that passes. We are what we are, let's not ruin ourselves, it's only life, our reality that passes on one side, it may be Arabic as speech but, at least it lives. It is always better not to remain without equal, when we are made false liars or, from being unclean things that will have an end. They make sovereign reign a dream substituted to the original one at the bottom, placed to reality then as you want, as you already know, but, don't remember they have forgotten you or, they have made you forget what you will soon remember, to believe again in that box, that base. Beautiful life exploited for the work of an ant, time is what is left before it goes out forever, you know kids don't have to use big words, when the world has already been for good. Things you don't say, novelties that ruin, nothing is true, everything is new every day so the new, the youngest. The world is fossilized in its form, making sure you always discover the same things, so living a world of dreams, instead of realizing a world of dreams. People make a world and a good, from things that you can not escape, a mirage is the dream understood, life just the fact that you go on, you do not know what is an unknown, the freedom to speak without offending.

So leave it alone, realize what you wanted then, do something else without cutting your veins there is always time ... where you put that damn book of instructions, an evil was going to kill you or make you commit suicide that was better, as serious as a plague without any kind of success, a cap to the idea. What wasn't supposed to exist or, something else associated with it that you don't want to pass off as common, is still there forever. Glory is forever, our life is marked, as it is today will not be tomorrow, they are thieves of ideas that no one wants to say, so as not to stain themselves with guilt for which they too are responsible. When people will do their own business! we need legislation that revolves the path of institutions, there are internal issues in every era, from which everyone can have their own profits and others that belong only to the generation in which you live, explanations that you can understand on your own, not organs and trumpets, but, situations that are already observed for some time now, are the most important then to succeed today from what you went through yesterday. Dreams are what you had to be today, having to be is the key to enter today's world. Serious morning of undated explanations, of uncertainties or improbable affairs, where the certainty is that the Sun exists. The streets are so many speeches at least two, do not believe the liars and mafiosi of the personality that say the world is theirs, even when the evidence there sees in the false.

An evil inflicts on us only life today, the emptiness in silence, in immobility. In one way or, only in another, what you were is what you will not be, it proposes a hidden good to life, where no one takes you and no one explains you. Prisons that want to seem or, to be freedom I see outside my windows today, not dry pasta dishes served in the streets. Words fall into the business that no one has ever illustrated, the dream of what was to be will be replaced, they say as soon as they get out of bed. All waxed with wax I mean, so to resemble a zombie, advice from a good party, a good homeland of the world from which you do not understand what nation we are, all confused between wrong opinions and, those perhaps.

No one can talk or other forms of degeneration, everything is wrong, chaos without order. I'm done for today, I'm out. Life is not a wheel and people are spaced out, circumscribed that the accounts are otherwise, do not stop at the appearance that is never obvious, what you see inside is the true appearance. They will try to hurt you, they will justify it as common peace or, because you are right. Staying still is the best of things in the worst case scenario, non-betrayal is the only guide to get out of this gain.

The unknowns and hypotenuse have never scared anyone, the triangle or the square are the first forms to resist the sinusoids of evil. The accounts always add up, the daily habits that are repeated in the day, the appointments with schedules, the days after form a rhythm that resembles life. Repeat so as not to fall but, not through the people in the company, the paradise in comparison is animal. Everything normal go and tell it to someone else, nothing is more normal, one day it will be coloured by new ideals never seen before, that was the normality, not that wrong being met or known, who keeps us together will have to give us explanations. A good is life or 'the paradise, continuing more within another reality or, original creature. What will ever be a mass unit to defeat at home, the hatred and tumult of things you don't understand... the grudges between people, that's all.

Tomorrow begins to play war at home, an irrelevant institution, true, as if defeating normality, was butter to slice. A rule doesn't exist, it tells you who doesn't live as a human being anymore, only after having defined some precise rules, even if they work, you can live peacefully the rest of the day, doing nothing. Pause returns to the initial position, peace of mind: getting lost without what. They will be concerns of the Municipality, sorry but what do you think you are, if not only important medicines to heal.

I feel like an old box abandoned or sealed, I've been sick, I've had a fever. Only a little blue, green or yellow sun tells me with courage there will be better days, you will suffer less, maybe because we have done it before.

It's getting late, bye.
Greetings G.

9.
The Hippocratic War

30.04.2008

"What you are will not become, that's the fake truth, Okay! But the future is the most wonderful thing man has to possess."

Too many restrictions, the world wants a lot of freedom, the news and the institutions have only to say, in my opinion is that little problem not to mention, not to get the damage. Problem on difficulty cannot be solved because you are the one who, or I the chronicle of the fact that it has never been interesting, are just prejudices for them, while the story begins in relation to the social dear. What remains is what is said, it doesn't matter, it has nowhere to explain itself.

Solutions have no body, only where they are described, they are explained, a poor denunciation would be good for everyone. A software to arrange things in order has already been created, everything has already been, all software, an intellect only deals with already existing objectivity, it is as strange as it may seem, what we are missing was not ours. Creation in general is a basis for escaping the trap of what is not ours: it is not our property, it is not our fault. Solutions may be in the past, an invention is something quite different from an unhealthy practice, from malware software. A memory rupture happens in time, a small sign is that you only have to think about the error in general, what was supposed to arrive has already happened, they tell us to wake up then, you see the others or, the biggest people sleep on speeches, projects never realized, what was supposed to be their own reality, to remain a dream.

Life is the present day, there's nothing left, that dilemma can't be solved and, we have to make do with it, this happens. Here they have already stolen from us all the envious, where all our money spent on public works will end up, it's never a place to settle one's soul as a rule. The world is its use or, our address, public or private bodies, lost causes and disused objects. Legal realities we don't know, eyes we don't have. The end is blurred, the voice lost in millions of other voices but, we remain waiting. Problems, chaos, state doubts, the expression lost in the common denominator, you can no longer see reality, because what we have done, we would not have built it. Fear of the unconscious is stronger than words and deeds... Fascism is security, the source from which there is no problem, the only solution or, light to follow in case of very large or insuperable issues, you know, it seems to me that 'the question does not look like a solution at home, careful who speaks, what they bring us is what will remain, they have never understood, they never will, they are against the eyes of people who do not believe them, you don't have to say anything they won't do anything to you, but if you want you should be.

Here not only the end of the world has come, the last solution has also passed, still nothing is down with strong manners, that people don't have ears to listen to, the truth has only one way, don't believe you hear it... it was just air, still nothing will see the light of a new day, then it was a good thing to kill or, the losses who don't know them, is the absurd. A good is a thought or, an action as forbidden as it is duty to perform, it can no longer be achieved, we took it away with the order.

There are natural antivirus, those who exist in the good live and that's all, they do everything with norm and calm, then lie down at the end, that there are no other problems. Substances and elements are the solutions to those problems that nobody solves. They were the thieves in mathematics, the friends of before, only it was not understood as soon as possible, if studying Dante will be enough to remain a good thing. There is still a mountain to climb, to get to the top, you must always do it yourself, no one will do it for you, in fact there are people who work to make you forget the work you have already done, that you are nobody, someone must know you and whoever succeeds must escape, you know, let's take a break. See if you can find some resistance, maybe in the fridge or if you can avoid that guy, there is still no account of how great that function was that they have not yet solved, then in the background was really a virus, and yet someone thinks about it, damn mosquitoes.

We are also Americans not only Italians, not only fashion, let 'time brings it, time washes, time does everything. They wouldn't let us stay here anyway, which was good for who? Anyway, if one day you connect up somewhere, you'll see the world hasn't lost its colour, it's above all freedom, doing everything by the book... maybe that's why I didn't graduate, don't think that that group is in order, a good thing is only you or all the others. Leave it, let them not decline yet, a good at most is an artefact, the created a product, there is what does not exist or the need, then the candy, the other things let's leave them alone. I'm going to eat, bye.

Continuing a speech has always been an exemplary diversion, if not an excellent solution to perform or, overcome all the unhealthy. The world is a ruin today, dear gentlemen in the day nine April zero eight there is no real system, whole from which to take full support, are just structures a good, a base is a base, you can only believe what you have, not what you had to have. In that place the escape has nothing to do with it, on the other hand it was just a waste of time, reality comes out only from passages that bring light, you get by applying the truth to creation, only by going the right way you get to the place where you wanted, you had to or, was going to go. There is only one way or, mode to have the price of life, compared to what we must have then is also what is needed. Breathing drives only what is needed, what we do not have is sometimes superfluous, liar. I think, I am.

You will see the solution to these uncertainties is always the same, the many people are not always those but, after all, what happens on duty, this tells me that, whoever arrives will be able to live in the good, who cracks, who leaves, will not be. You will see who will know only the true, and eliminated the error, attacking what is not right will always be better than staying without the air gained, better than stealing. It is a torment that has reigned through the centuries, of putrefaction of the flesh and spirit, to be dissipated always every day, without making so many problems.

An evil must not happen ... it is already a good result, it must be repaired, built. The world has never been finished, you need to make a long race, to appear in the kingdom of heaven alive these days, you can reach beyond, it will also be true that bad people are really evil, the classic rhetoric is evil, even from centuries back to this, so you will see that famous spiral cone, placed behind you.

What works is already working, don't think you're making money alone in law, you can build as many buildings as you want, those built next to yours are already ready and inhabited, what bothers you is who builds on the sea or on the shoulders of others. The speech is its continuation, where a speech ends one could deal with one's personal and interpersonal tasks, the end of a speech has already begun while you were thinking about what you wanted to say. The end has already begun with the birth, don't forget that you need it.

Only an indication should always be given is a momentary need, a duty not to forget, not to forbid or ignore, the road lights up. Resurrecting is only what is good, so we will miss one day, there is no other solution, after all it is only a living human interval ... after purgatory, uh, paradise then all to work, hoping to still be alive with dignity and dignity, without excessive trouble as today, start again this infected sea.

The ruin is a starting point, only for very strong people are believers in God, not all of us are familiar with the mafia or other homemade things. The accounts come back from symmetries of a function, we have not made the creation of us, we are part of it, it's more a matter of comfort, living like wearing a dress but, never that of evil, because they go to hell. Leave a detail in your constitution of objects, to see the base, the desk, the floor these days it is said that you see us double, instead we are people without documents uh, updates or, what you want to be, still do not understand what is real from what is false, people seem to rejoice in hell.

A notification is never bad, the writing is good

even if not in your eyes but, of those who can look or, the opposite, the rest will be future, if not our of those who will come. That enormous mountain of what we are not, the denial of life will have to be defeated, no one takes the place of another, what we are depends above all on us but, the world is not all ours, our conscience but, even that of those who do not work is taking the money that does not belong to them, we are all responsible for a state problem that was wrong is still wrong, at most you see what you have to do with it.

The future happens with great simplicity, it seems but it is not true: who is safe in our days is only God, they will return to them and, their accounts, stories, are parasites, worms, viruses, malignant as yet will be the fault of the state if you do not see well, not a lack of you, no fault is yours, there are no people who are to blame, those are thieves who want to say: it's me.

You should already know this maybe, they do us evil on purpose... but you haven't seen anything, have you? You've seen that nobody does anything, in error and cruelty, maybe you don't know what the penalty is, so it's easy. The State doesn't have for everyone, it's just fantasies, graffiti, you come when you can or, when you have to, more adult people or, who knows, smaller people, there's nothing left that isn't possible, but to understand all the offenses by yourself is one thing to do.

Only holes, they would be today another part of what you had to know or, what they didn't tell us, you will do what you can do, in this place without human targets, from derivations and sources in a built world. Isn't the first source of love called death, isn't it in life? All roads built on evil are wrong, short or long, the majority are false, who wants to take you away. They used to say when I was a boy who wasn't there, won't be there. I hide the things you can't know, what you are part of, jackals of good on humans who then want to be confused for good people, repeated acts that are part of sections of the world already seen, they must not realize fear but, scrutinized then leave them.

Another of these days is coming to an end, even more is to be understood that meaninglessness leads to nothing or, that sometimes it has already been lived, structured what should still succeed, to arise is to see the sunlight without dazzle. In the clear you can see better, it is always from there you have to start, in the day there is night and in the night there is day, it is not true! We must instead separate, divide to know individually all the ele-ments, the end you have already understood it is said but, when is it no or how much we are now? It still seems another day and the past is a thing to throw away like garbage but, that I remember remains without the precise sizes, you have to hold on to the bus is not to lose anything so worrying, as the background is said to lose your life.

We reorganize again in five minutes... nothing has happened yet? What do you want me to say is the dead man playing at another theatre or, a play of guards and thieves. You finish the games, people stay, theories are associated with reality, without any smear, you can't live everything, life is a dream you have to know how to fall and many other little things you don't have to, like getting stolen not to lose. It is thought that we do not fall into the form suitable for living, we fall into our source that 'the trunk of our body. He says there will be no more good, the fellow goes to hell, indeed he has not yet done so. An education is higher than what it was, it resembles the walls of that institution which is so dear to us.

What it doesn't support today is the state! This environment is as big as the world but, not an enclosed space, you won't lose the taste of salt. Our home is also the world, it has openings towards all nations if you look at America on one side, Germany or France on the other, Russia and then the

East is not closed. I'm tired of writing but, I feel exceptionally well, then I conclude: if that hurts us goes in the memory, the arrests are studies already lived. Indigestion, fat intestine, come don't insist, eat that is clarified, they are wars of saints, nobody has ever fooled us, who shoots is shot.

Today I feel much superior to the problem of the false, not even in the theatre. After all what is 'the true taste of peace, not disturbing the peace, the absolute certainty of being alive, if never close the walls of the earth's borders, where you could be, instead of finding yourself in another city, you always need a hand, how to leave the thought where it is instead. What you see on your belief is your limit, nothing can explain it to you, there are laws written, others are things, that are not here where we are, that dust is evil.

In fact, the leaders are a bit confused, they are always the ones from sources to causes, when that day comes that will be the fault, those are the guilty ones, nothing is stolen, no one takes the place of another, people are wrong, like the environment on the other hand.

It's loneliness among us on the other hand, as if you don't do it no one will do it where you are, the same is true for everyone, no one will ever do anything, until we are called to bring the good we have, no one will ever know, no one is said, no one has to see it. Let's remain calm here there is no one but, they want us to arrive when everything is over or, when someone will be gone, we will arrive after not going back, because there is no going back. What you don't say hurts sometimes, you don't run away from trivial things are the law, life sometimes. It will be a new light, you don't lose anything, the loser is already far away. It is a vertex that draws us downwards, the universe that surrounds it, is formed in dull natures and laws already written, from registers where evil is easy to nest, thus creating a retrograde world without God, at least in active presence. Hell for those who don't like it is always a point of arrival, from emptiness on the planet or, from one planet to another, then we talk about epochs between us that divide tens of years into one or, what can one still expect when one is over thirty.

Human beings look like shells, it seems as if they are eaten there, always playing these big ones, just play there is life there, beautiful present as a picture in a mirror to cross. Those who don't exist are gone, they are no more, the end. Who can after us, be sure who arrives calls! A perfect image limitedly equal to our citizens. Hello again to resent in a thousand years yet, moved to unequal environments, because the parties are not at peace with each other, nothing happens until we are together, just a beautiful mist, where we see nothing, only what we have stolen or, what is not yours that you cannot take advantage of, to become better.

Only the dead can improve what nonsense, remember the offense is a tool that is imprisoned to understand the best things, if you want answers are within us ... as the years that have passed, we spend together with the time we occupy. What you are, you write it or rather you do it... not what they tell us to be, but what we are here, in that place over there, then there is almost nothing outside. Of this time, of this era, everyone writes and stays in their places, a good thing is our memory of today, as in ten years from now I would see it, it is always necessary to make assessments of what happens to find the origins, the functions to then think about something else, being here is not to be bad, all together always.

It's already afternoon don't believe that the speech would have solved anything, there are many interferences, it's a matter of remaining silent, don't get much help. Ok, maybe it's already late but, you can't even imagine how much, it's other people's business our life, maybe it will be better understood later or when? The past events have passed, the future instead, it's a huge shining mountain, don't peel your knees, go on down your way, if you still see ahead there will be many trees still to be observed and, castles inhabited by famous people or warriors already dead for a long time. I wish you a life of happiness, what life is for. Beautiful, full of problems without a way out, without mortal problems, without even thinking about it anymore, take the gun and shoot yourself, I'm joking... how many things you do without leaving a mark, you will rarely remember them but, in the background, they don't only serve to fill the holes in your memory. On the contrary no one declares the true truth, it's what you should pass for neglect, so you lose the true sense of ideas and, people where to go to try to live again. It happens that what is needed is thrown away, the goals are just a mirage and, people do not know what to work.

The facts have been forgotten, the strongest wins, he commands. What you believe is not yours, they gave it to you, while that impossible life form of yours secretly corrodes our souls, sometimes it's just habit the rest. I know that it's everyone's business: no one expresses himself with open forms, what success really is, what happens. We are no one, others live elsewhere even in evil, the play says, but there is a part of truth that is what they have stolen, it is certainly won but, we do not want to believe, as there is a good and healthy form of depersonalization. They are just false fascists and parasites, let's hope it goes well, have a good evening.

The weather is clear, the day looks good, a good is always stronger, a bad is wrong. A good has already won, who hasn't won, has already lost. Fear is what remains, not what you have left, nothing bad remains. A speech is common, until you find your way home, after you have imagined closing the door of it. Of need and people in need, you need to be thirsty, to feel the quality of life and to realize that you are still alive.

This is the end of a new epilogue, an embrace G.

10.
Recycling action

31.05.2008

"To live with the certainty, to be mathematically extinct."

A good thing is when we arrived or, when we have nothing to do at all, everything is already built, we will walk and from there we will be. Tomorrow doesn't exist, but at least we'll be there, it's another thing to sleep. Sweet sleep while the year runs of such bets or, losses even just thunderstorms, you always think the best, that 'the worst already past. In the end it could not be just a problem from oral expression, more than anything else you think of crossing a good, but as always you do not pass, is a scale not a right, otherwise what was all that heaviness, all the tragedies do nothing but dramatic work.

In some time you'll feel better, it's not a form of racism, say it or think it, whoever thinks about betrayal has failed, is a failure. You live not in that place or somewhere in particular but, everywhere, how the step of the return goes. What you are not, you will not be to go without losing, what you have on. In the return of things and ideas, a bigger model is created, history makes us great but, not that treacherous coffee that says today is already past, tomorrow is yet to come.

Nothing in thought stops, you can't reset life. Modern life is really varied in our days, we have to choose what can better identify what we wanted, there is always the need to do something, the need to decide which things or people are good, nothing comes randomly then, there will be objectivity that we do not understand, the rest is better not to tell. Use the right way or, the right quality, we say all thoughts are problems, addictions are already decided or prescribed, as what can happen is already known in reality. A good is born only within precise rules, from which you cannot escape, our product is what the light of the eyes is trying, from ten minutes before, is only a surface what is wrong. It may well be a discourse that continues, not by itself all this or, the power to know what stops us. Now all that lived until today, is what can happen tomorrow, how this enters us, and it is us. The rest is what not everyone has done, or a way of counting when you subtract. Poverty in words makes us, he understands us, takes the people who lied to us, uh, betrayed us to jail. In Italy it's not very fashionable, look back to see what they have already stolen from you, you have to stay still but not motionless, nobody dies, who leaves life has already been chosen, like who has to live, time is a measure, these will be public mental slowdowns. The whole of existence to choose who must live, making a move is forbidden, you did not know gruff! otherwise they can remove us from the register where we are enrolled. Beauty is forbidden, normal is accepted, only what is the arithmetic history of facts and successes.

Me and my car have always been friends for the skin... the rest was just a surface or, from which side you go out, you need to make a hole to see if there is the Sun on the other side, a declaratory act avoiding disgust and, embarrassment. There is an alphabet, an association of ideas to be out of that trouble, which this afternoon, will present us as the final solution, which completes life is what you cannot refuse or deny. How many ideas and objects are forbidden today, like thoughts looking ahead from a high wall, where some arrive on tip-toe, others are unable to overcome.

Living better is like existing without harm, the expression, the words that nobody says, and then you return almost as before, always the same things, the same people but time passes, the period, the important thing is to recycle everything, people sometimes go away and, objects are consumed. One time it is to see the light to begin with, another time to relax, where there is no longer the problem that everything wanted to take but, not everything is ours, it is written at the entrance of the city. We look like imperfect wrecks at home, we need to commit our own good in society to keep nothing, to use what is abstract for us and for everyone. Time wears us down what has happened? life created by the system that was evil in truth, it seems a structure that moves our impressions, wants our decisions or, what we are in greater part, look I tell you, we would like to present evils today, as if they were our watches. Always listen to your heart and good music. Maybe they are plastic or wax, poor sick people, then rich after all look at your face you should find that you have lost nothing, when you have nothing more, you died at this game. Yes, it's certainly you, what they're looking for but they'll lose, but don't always think badly it's you that or that place you had to do or, call someone is you didn't do. Our life is a software package of implementations already understood, that no one has explained to us, we are in one way is not in another, you can and you cannot do things, as many are already resolved undeclared, it would depend only on applying them. A near future will only be a realization of what in theory, it is already explained clearly, you don't have to be surprised about anything, just the letter Y, no sound or new idea, an image, a present music is not a void.

What you could do if you didn't know it, then you didn't do it, realized neither you nor who you know. What we lack, that's what they erased from us but, so we won't be at the bottom, we don't have to argue with anyone, it's just a problem of presence, something that the eyes or, the others solve, maybe it's serious what we still have to do, still the bells instead of the huts.

We are kept in a bottle with a screw cap, so we stay until the good weather, do not believe it he never wins, it is the future that is coming with that air of the past, an evil no longer knows who he wants to fool, a common thought, a common malaise is not what. Society is an ice cream to eat or, a full of mistakes and things done badly, you have to go right at the bottom, consolidate that 'the point further down then, ask for information to continue. Easy true, you have to study but, it is also true that books must sometimes have distances of many kilometres, from where we are. It's lunchtime to whoever you want to tell, I've always said that evil must be exploited, its unhealthy philosophy. Giving yourself a start is one of the most difficult things but, it is better to decide what flavour to taste, after growing up it becomes a different way of being.

Mutilations to be different from what, by norm built daily we should be, it's a game for children to get lost or, even for adults? it's fundamental to believe, there are things now, that are not just for this day, we need to cut the air around us, to see what exists, then we will get out. It always seems the same thing but, I've seen and I don't think that this would be all that could ever happen, causes and inefficiencies create a chaos wrong, even think there is a right chaos but it is of another of us. To give ourselves more freedom is to start eliminating things: folders, files, effects of use and other things, people who have nothing to say about us, because we will get out of this cage, there is no possibility of remaining in evil, deluded by a clause, at a point and time. Prepare yourself so much in the end, you won't see anything... laugh, only one rule is find or discover. What you want to know, you have to ask a lawyer. Better silence sometimes but, after having spoken enough, living dead differs from alive, a situation of passage that finds is crossing the road of life, who is not afraid that it could be living, being without all the diseases gathered to go away, lunch which is always a novelty.

The recycling of a life, the recalculation of probabilities. Seeing people again or, finding others, forgetting to start again for sure, to keep in training. Time passes by, that dream is not a dream but, the mathematical certainty of going to end up there, with no chance to escape. To enter a world then different from what you thought for sure, sometimes totally different, there is no such act in reality or, in its widest part, we are stronger than an illness but, because there was nothing in that place, it was only there.

Malaise is in the air, it was said in the early years of the year two thousand, a general non-personal discourse, of all people it was not built world, made up of small everyday problems. Only reports in a police station, under attack of evil, as what you can't say, the air was infected, where you went you found it present to stop a malaise, not instead of a good equal to the future, if you could go in the future, there was no discussion about this or that. A widely used principle was to avoid bad thoughts, karma was my fashion, a common thought that changes a fashion, a modernity is something else, as words really assure us presence, not from now on in time the past is a very important act, for today's history. An end does not exist is said peacefully, when the end has already happened, there remains a pile of rubble to wear to understand where you exit from, there is no exit we must stay here. Looking at the sunlight can be a side effect, the world is not ridiculous but past, lived for a long time, not even people are ridiculous, evils yes, are what they say are the modern era. They say there's always an exit, it's a solution, it's the need to breathe.

Nothing can be erased, the past is the imprint of your foot as you walk. Reconstructing is a practice that I see very positively, from good fruit both for the mind and for others, the basic recycling to remain alone and complete, instead of all alone with no way out, without the possibility of saying goodbye. My product was what I had done but, even with others, it's not true that you don't say, there are things you don't do. Open your eyes in front of everyone, we are not finished mountains, where to write the memories of a life or, rocks of finished thoughts, where to continue writing, for everyone then becomes a lake, where you do not live life, water has a taste.

A memory is not to want evil anymore, to take it inside, not to run away anymore, to reinforce it is to believe in the law, in people who are not part of our centre. What do you want me to say, tell me never say, without a reason. Whatever happens to us, don't ask for too many explanations, you won't get what you want, but it's our wrong instinct, or the mistake that everyone has made. Don't worry, you won't get it, because they are owls who swallow the unhealthy even in front of you, right? They're instruments of torture and pestilence. Words that have ruined the life you won't have, surely you have to go back to the law, recycled endlessly in the memory, that an evil goes somewhere. An evil is over, or ends there is no doubt, go the road is free further ahead, but the other part of you does not exist, you will not have it, there is nothing worse than a state of transition, as he arrives everything is erased, it does not exist, uh, you cannot be different, I give you some advice if you want to eliminate it now. La belle époque, they didn't explain themselves, people keep on flowing, while the city burns, nothing exists between us, it was just the absence of that speech, a software of all things, that we will solve later.

It's nineteen thirty-five and I've finished working, I don't know what I'd like to do, I'm going to the gym in a little while, it's evening, there's not much left to do but think about you or, to invent that I don't have more than that, is to complain that I've already finished. It's better to speak directly, I've always spoken directly and correctly... it's more difficult to do than to say, don't think about the negativity that is part of the evil, that life always smiles at you.

Bye, G.

11.
Words that cannot be used

30.06.2008

Asleep, asleep without knowing why, nothing worse exists except loss of memory or intellect. The rest dedicated to living after the passing is an evil, ignorance that wants to defeat the conscience, people lost, lost with no way out for not wanting to eliminate it, but, the sky is covered with absurdity and, the earth seems a flying saucer that moves making us swing, nothing fear the communion dissociates the bad from the good, creates what he does not want.

Never come out of evil, the roads are like highways, so many countless that you can go to many different places. Words, amplification plus other good things, are the ways not to remain in the darkness of the mind, to live better, remember for us as children, it was a common project the strength to inflict, the life of human beings who have very little human but, they were liars and sac-rileges around us, and it's all fraudulent, mediocre even now but, it's not a fake whole, as 'l black, white is really. What concerns us happens in ten years not now, everything had already happened or, will happen in the future but far from us. Who does not believe is a nonsense, try to go out with-out you, some things are different from what they are, you need to believe/know, everything was al-ready past but will come again, even if not com-plete as before, then we will do something else. To live the world is to believe but, if I told you that hell exists out here, it's not believing in the help of others, in the police, in the State that still remains in the things we don't have. Put a sticker on the false one, keep going, you have to move forward, what is a bubble of ignorance if not an evil, we don't believe we are you.

In the distant place where you will read these pages like here, it is useless to write about things you will not know or see, because they will be erased but, as you can get lost in a mistake that lasts two weeks continuously the same, we are lost and that is already everything. What you feel is already all that is possible, your whole life is all that you see, what you are, what they have done to you... pray I am another. Now it's evening, peace the solutions have already arrived, those who were attentive understood, all the others did not, it will be the State's fault if you have no eyes, organize the dinner is the fault of loneliness. Lately if you look for people in Italy, you have to find them in an ice-cream, you think you are going to die but, as it is difficult to stop living, then you are not there.

A cage, a cube are things to say, lost in a mountain of ideas, wrapped with newspaper and things to do. Differences between things and people, words that you can't use, all you have to do is good, after sure somewhere, comes the solid money that is yours. In this world of imagination if you don't speak, you will never know what or who you are, all the confusion for a mathematical certainty, which guarantees afterwards you will be paid. Certain realities are the ones to follow, to stay here, the rest do the others do not believe, what is left does not say, there is nothing, where you can get tonight, the games have already been ruined. They are exaggerated evils, the world is like a wall because you cannot continue, there is only air and the road, where you meet the end of the toys is also in another way.

A mistake in person is already seen that says nothing ... we are the ones in the video, whose life is that if not ours. Maybe the boys have not focused a disintegration of limbs, organic functions, the supply of food, if you want peace, the end, life, you have to fly to a person without understanding anything about her, never laugh in someone's face, otherwise they arrest you. Thoughts that don't end are life, others that can't steal from us are us, an ideal opening is just a game of inexperienced people, death is a wickedness, they didn't know how it happened in particular that fact or who and where, nobody must know what is in the evil, not everything is already decided, it could be a future our lack not to go out, it's a dream the rest.

It's yours what's left of us, not this nightmare to demagnetize, with the law and us. You remember a good thing, it wasn't a dream but, they're where they are... and we had almost nothing to do with it, you just have to smile at evil, no changes have been made to yours, theirs and mine in any way, but they still have to "do" a good or the good. Be careful in realizing, not to produce thoughts or actions legally malicious or unhealthy, think about what you wanted to know about fascism, you have to realize on your own, imprison yourself and imprison yourself, in front of everything. Listen usually they already wanted to do it to us, or the opposite, do not tell me that you do not want to attack them, always look at the spy light you see, afterwards they will let us know how this sentence ends.

Make of flour, make an album a song, where you lose people, where they end up is better to say, even to do that! Where you have not gone well, speeches that from a certain point of view, do not fit the normal use of common words, where there is no longer good, what a doctor can tell you, what we can or, we cannot do is decided by law, even what is real or false, is nobody called the law first and then. You, Mr. and Mrs. are not what many artists think your vein, they are just what you can do, what a lawyer or the police can do. Turn your thoughts to them too, you'll see the problem solved, it's not true that there is no solution, call a specialist technician.

It is the institutions, the reforms that carry out what we believe. We are the institutions, the rest is only in a lost point but, it is a place with a dynamic public ip, an identified base. Dante, Carmelo Bene, the prefecture, the ice-cream shop, the mixture of this finally becomes unity or, it becomes nothing, unity is the end. Life is not only this or that but, a harmony of acts that form thought and good things, it still seems to be ahead then lost, it seems to be erased, it no longer exists, no memories have been erased, how much work there is still to do. The world we came from, it is a resurgence on one side, everyone has gone where? there is no one left here. There's more lost, believe me, not what we shouldn't have said we were. Never heard of inferior beings, in another way you don't know you are superior, to those things that are not people. When you're constantly beaten, someone wakes up and goes to sleep, you don't have to accept America and then they say they're finished! There was no motivation, instead there was a good thing, where no one is left, a flower is born.

In the end we finish, do you have any other topic tonight? we need is what if we have already eaten, you all have our seats graduated and state. Without problems where the realities are, many people say, that missing wall is not everyone's, only who is without finishing the sentence. An arithmetic to find the keys to the house, recognize all the people and objects in the street even tomorrow, if you do something wrong there is the possibility that you kill yourself, what could be the worst, hell is not ours, for millennia we have been working not to go to hell, we need to see things outside, we are how many things there are out there, in addition to those that now you have to avoid. In the end, don't run away and get caught even when you're young, because it's all over long ago, if you don't know. Good things that no one says or rather repeats, or prays to. Everything is over, but if you listen to an evil you become an ugly person! Some things have never been erased, the future for example, if we have been arrested, then there is no future. You know arrests, evil beings, things you don't say, things you don't do. Everything is accomplished, Jesus Christ says so. A good thing is the next day, still forbidden in Italy but, the rest is the same, we are still forbidden, who thought to rule in peace, in harmony, on this day of the end of the war, after what will be, it is said that no one has won but, there will not be another game.

Words sometimes end, what you can say is sometimes very little, if you do not make a difference between the uncertainties of all and the problems. The questions of the good are everyone's concerns and, the problems of the State, then so it is not true that the State has no problems, a good thing is us, we do not mean today so tomorrow there will be no more, there is always a sort of bigger door, where to go knocking.

It's true that it can take a bit of experience, but there are different ways to savour the life that is her, you can even watch her from a window, while no one touches her or, already you have eaten what is called everything. Stories of our life are the future, when you feel left you'll know, even here no one has done anything, who have fun and do not solve it, just because it was bigger than expected the trouble, they could not know I am everything or, other things that have already taken away from the good. It's better to rest in a comfortable situation, they have accepted an evil, while some people around keep the others who have not, pushed too far forward society is maintained because the bad things still live, but you have to prune what is everything, if it is the time. Where nothingness is the greatest, we don't want to see, we are on our way to a happier world, without those people or, those objects that we can't accept, like the dysfunction created and other stories for those who don't live or, who don't want to make live, when we still have to overcome that fantasy but, we are only creative energy like the light of the electric current, there are realities that are not discussed, you with those must have frequent relationships.

People do not overcome themselves, vulgar things are uglier than what they say then, it was not a time of jokes and jokes or, of a bedlam of who was, there are laws that you do not overcome, is to think that the guilt was to be a human or, believe to have been classified or, to live in a prison. Pho-bias are a prison, those who have escaped don't know, those who don't want to resurrect.

Other people's problems are none of our busi-ness, all solved is that they don't know to whom or where to turn. Problems, solutions are business for the people who use them, we still postpone that speech that had to be made, I think everyone will have said that someone else did it, and then we still get confused by trivial things. They are all sick, nobody is to blame. Forms of pure madness to overcome, it's better not to say the others. The sun will warm us and then you'll feel the beauty, never say what you didn't want to say, it's his fault.

A hug G.

12.
The day of the rat is its death

31.07.2008

Calmness is the virtue of the strong, a calm to proceed, so much so that one does not pass through, nothing ends, nothing exists in the void. From the good one does not go out, except through a door, one cannot say that it is the end, it remains a problem that is done in the meantime, and there are always those who forbid doing and do not understand. Hopefully not to die, is to keep talking as long as you can, even in an absurd tomorrow out of what should be, what is forbidden you do not know, just to live in the heat or, do not continue to suffer, go out, run away, die. A good is not an exaggeration, not all out then all inside, you owe respect for the law, it's yours or, really it is better not to continue that speech or fact, which is to do something else. Everything is possible, nothing is feasible, are diseases even of this modern era, of which I have news. Everything you said before is true, wait for its time, it happens in the future, talk to the original people in your photographic image, the other past things, the speeches of people who have lived with you in the past years, then it comes out what it should be for what it seems to us.

The law governs undisputed what 'the past, you need to cut those threads that do not serve, one day the evils will disappear without difficulty. Summer is near, the heat is a friend of good and honest people, it will be the years and the time that will change our lives, there are spaces where the visual concept of life can be very strange, do not continue to do, which is better than not. Where is the peace on this planet, issues too big seem false, vast problems never been solved, the sea is evil, while houses, colours is all that included already ready, I still know that ailment, the stain true and delinquent, that forces us, steals us even the day, it is with this you must not make mistakes, it is we who must survive otherwise uh, ahead of time. Yeah, they didn't explain it well, you can't live in mid-air, without explanations about human decency. Every past is already understood, you want me to show you the thoughts of people these days, the closures and doors never opened, the things that go through too many difficulties, they always say it's not just my business, sometimes it's none of my business at all, you know? Power games on our skin, what is the purpose of their practices, who really gains, where are those beads thrown for a long time is lost now, they offend a good, so many things are already lost for years.

Economic forces applied to time as a conquest, for me they are property of rats for power, a robbery of rats in everything, worse than that there is nothing but this: evils continue endlessly but, in a concrete way what is an evil, a rat, a finite when you talk about it. It expresses its dead form, then if you don't finish it you are not free, come on I didn't do it to you, that's how things stand, not lying down, definition is perception, if you take care of those people you'll find them shattered. The world is fascist in order to fight fascism, anyway a gun or a complaint was better, I suggested but they were happy.

Too many freedoms do not free, too many constraints and lightness from everyone, but the evidence escapes, as the reality always remains the same. A good is a cathedral, it has no slopes that are not its own, an evil is that rat, the rest is the difference. Bells are opinions, music is music like other things identified in our state, which trembles like a leaf, knows but what the modern day wants, the day of the rat is its death. Our family members are not in evil, they have been closed beyond, with all the qualities but nothing is known about it, nothing has been solved, a good not me at least in part but almost all humans, they suffer from wars that are also in small part of them and partly associated with them, you do not know who is associated for our evil. A good doesn't close, it doesn't end, we disappear one by one, new units are always born for life, the truth will always be known, don't kill yourself for a product that will come in the future, in the meantime do something else. In this moment we are all on earth and nothing can change our end, perfect but preferably also our ends, live free life in the good, a dream that escapes today.

Remember, a part is material and a spiritual always, neither of the two can certainly be omitted to live free lives. To the people who say we have already solved do not believe it, we do not have a news bulletin or a poster, nothing if you want on what really interests us, except what is the common interest of the person. The money hasn't been taken away, we'll do well: the month, come on, it's the future you want, you can take away someone false if you stay alive, some things you don't say.

Today is a new day, in a hurry I have to leave in five minutes, my kidneys are still working and how many memories, I live on memories, of the past. I feel of that problem as a distant day, as today a distant recurrence, they have not cut the present with the past, it is the future as a whole, there is no voice that guides us out of reason, from you, from me in this moment, instead the calculations, the bases, the hypotenuses to make the existence disappear, which then are also me or you.

I repeat to you is in common language the evil, exists not understood is our neighbour or, three streets under what you have to eliminate. They wanted to steal everything, they told their friends that they had done it, that they had taken everything, then in reality nothing is legal for them, in fact at this time of the evening there is harmful, everything they had taken has dissolved. Conscience, Ave Maria. Here look on the other side that's a good thing, an even greater good, they say what you have done or, they will do once you enter here will be satisfied.

There is nothing if a good is later, they paid you go buy what you wanted, then it's yours. Zombie, uh zombie is dead alive not nowhere, all things are affected by the mountain of what you do not know or, they did not tell you, to get where people say tomorrow, there is so far away that not even in a year you get there. No one has ever told us that it can arrive tomorrow what the same is not reached that at least in a year, it is a practice carried out according to rules that you do not know, I know how, just the day of tomorrow, it will be forbidden to have, the forbidden will be just what was needed to breathe tomorrow, it will be necessary to find some solution, here the forbidden realities are so many that almost makes me laugh. They even go so far as to say that you don't have to talk is all fake, less often that you are a fake, that is to say it's all true but you didn't know that there was even a god in evil, a monstrous animal uh, a cockroach. You have to let it pass, it goes away, without giving it much consideration, it means nothing to talk to it except to hit it.

Usual problems that one day will be solved, don't you think? In my opinion even today, it is in what era you live Christian future, you must demand from your technology that you have, they say today is all possible. Everything already has a name, it's enough to find out, that is, tomorrow go and see, many and many things are there and nobody uses them. Problems are problems, remember they are objects that if you don't solve them will eat you up, sometimes don't think about them but look and pass. Yes, it's true it's more difficult than it seems but, I can already see very honest solutions for where to rest today, then it's just a state of passage, so shorter than a normal life, how could you stay in evil and a burnt youth, like how old are you? fifty.

Living outside you say, you go and live in a meadow, you think you're a party and I make people laugh, always the same story then if you look ahead at the bottom you see the pension, then the end. They've won, they've killed you, you laugh but, I mean, you left him. Now who is in charge of those issues, if not even a lawyer lives the good, diseases that they say we cannot do now, we must end up making way for the new winner, younger. Fascism is not low league or false, there is still debate in Italy, whether it is right to live or die, you know what I usually do, I listen to music to solve. Working is always a good game for you, they've already done it, now they tell you. You see they didn't call it right, they didn't even see it from too much fog, maybe from too bad on and around. I wanted to tell you don't pick up the sound wave without the noise of the Earth, it's not a distributor where you can get the news that thing, even if you want to be malicious, it would be much better to avoid absorbing its good and other evening fantasies. You spend without understanding almost nothing, just that street where you do not end up not to be alone, we will find again that order must be in its place at the bottom of that closet, in your first home ... of course they have already done so but where were we, it would be better to have another coffee but, I think it's already late and the circumstances are already very confused, do not rhyme than to entrust the evening to fate, stop talking, hold your nose. In normal life there is an evil hidden, but when everything and everyone is in life normally. Enemy of normality, I will be where she will no longer be, will be the eye of the evil duplicate along with other things or, a world that continues to do that should do, because it is so. Where not to go, it's not explained, you have to know, one knows what he had to know but, what they stole, what you wanted to do and they won't let you do it seems to me more difficult, one rebels at what height one travels, where humans are broken up the world has disappeared but, you'll see it will reappear further down the road.

Perverts, memory killers. Prisons in the prison, is many legal realities not used for the right way,

only the emptiness, what flavour has the emptiness, look what they have produced people without image, a false silence, recover you can always
but, the damage who pays there. It is thought that
those who are in contact with that idea live in the
bottom, in reality they are nonsense, they bump
into people who have become sensitive. A law is
always right but the simple one, like the fundamental nature, then I am interested in the fact that the
objects will explain themselves.

The expression is everything, I guarantee you,
that function is already solved, it is not understood
… it is already solved do something else exponent,
there is the need for what? If you don't believe in
an old power, it's in all the great things to defeat.
Huge mountains of questions, they are in the future the children's games, but now they are problems that not even the State solves.

Have a good summer vacations, bye G.

13.
The fact that it wasn't me,
it wasn't you...

East, summer 08 - 31.08.2008

It seems to work better, after this installation lasted a day, cute even my new notebook, as the expected can last for a long time, I will also buy a leather case, if it keeps like today. I'll wait the next days to try it, I don't believe it yet but this thing works, a precious object must, it will work with just one installation is new, black, to distinguish it I have a dvd to start again then, I go to the ATM to compensate dad. It's okay the second time... the use is all normal, the applications, internet and Bluetooth.

Tomorrow is what it was supposed to be, I remind you, you didn't have any desire to travel, but instead you go back to where you stay so you don't fall. It works like this: here you change from day to day, even if for me the game is already over, ask again about the state where there is no state or there is no state says who is wrong. Where we are not is where we have not yet arrived, landed, matched with the ground but, without staying in mid-air. It's true who knows, doesn't know what, doesn't know about accidents, inconsistencies, un-visited places, illnesses, memory loss and, even more what is yours, will never be again. Those who think that there is still an evil in our days, when there is only evil and boredom, where we are lost is that we will never be again, instead those who believe in the government as healthy in everything have only to go further away, to see who they have struck for the umpteenth time, without fault and reason, in any case here is all serious, weighs as much as no one realizes their due, there are those who believe that they have not managed to finish a deal, which in part is not even his. Tomorrow I will leave for the holidays in search of peace and serenity, fish and sea.

By now I'm on vacation, it's 7:02 a.m. is Sunday with the usual rebuses! life and opportunities, as always could have been in a completely different way, then I think they are the reversals of what they are now. Explaining or trying to explain is a waste of time, or the truths, people have to understand them on their own, they are never alone. Their evil... worse, they don't see, they don't hear, they don't see, they don't hear while the older ones say to continue on our way which is better, great full of important people who will come to them along its paths. It would be useful to explain I think, after all, the people I met in the bus will also have a reason, it seems they do not know what reality is but, looking better they do not know when it happens, it will be the quantities that move our politics and the economy in general. Not being like non-existence, they are the same for everyone like flour. In the past they are qualities, in those places or acts that many people have forgotten, they tell you this is what is not there. They are crimes during the day, while among us we were already talking about the heavens this morning, a good thing works as if you were alive, only here really. Food has a different taste, life is of a different colour and tone, what was said to be non-existent or false, instead is the only real thing, the world. The rest is boredom or, an act in the commission of a crime, a nothing but, that even in Italy I have known is studied, how not to look at the vulgar. Consider and overcome that bad scene, figure, act in any form or entity. Certain actions are not done, even if you can't see, at that moment because or what, they didn't cheat us, only a few people understand. It's a disaster, the soup is made of clay or Greta ... it seems all busy, a dreamlike vision then they made it stay like that you do not believe it, there is no good, then as suddenly it is in front of us or, it happens to meet him at five in the morning or five in the afternoon. Hunger doesn't happen on time, you still don't understand, they have to do it again, they destroyed it, they didn't like it, now it's their business, you don't believe in good, in the place where you live, you don't believe in the good, in the place where you live, you think that rebuses can't be solved anymore or, they've gone out of fashion, you just have to turn on the light then, find a reason to stay upright, don't see that strange guy anymore or, kind of idea that comes back, it's up to him, that state stop.

When you talk about a question, you almost always fall into a still life, a still life picture or, like in a movie. In the meantime time passes and, things get fixed, don't believe you, it's not just behind the front door the obstruction, the ruin of the world, without ruins you don't live, but what does it matter without light you don't breathe, without law you don't recover a house that burns or, it's burned. The absence of what was meant to be, one believes at home is the only master. The speeches are all over, now you are left without speaking, there is an order for all things, but if you do not use your conscience they do not work, it is true how men have been framed, there are habits that cannot be transgressed, the law governs all the objectivity that these people so funny, do not intend real. What's for lunch today, one shoots at everything and everyone or, intellect enters instead of oblivion, cause or effect. It melts like an icicle in the Sun, that dark monster but, it must be the law to take it away, it is a rat but it must be destroyed, it must pay everyone, everyone's business. We do not exist, we are ornaments of the house, I am going to have breakfast, the quality of life is never lost, from here we leave to arrive a good, a being of superior life. It seems to work, after all, it's where we live, it's who we are, the infection will disappear and we'll live again without anxiety, it's said where it no longer exists, there you are. Time doesn't matter, it will all be over, not incomplete, a finished job, without things to do yet, everything in its place.

Good evening, a few words just to tell you, it's not better to see each other again tomorrow, without neglecting being and becoming, so they can seem absurd... nice relaxing, warm evening, I met some people. Inside this film who says the words end is the story as well, it's not true, the arguments are consumed, nothing really ends, the use one does things determines the state of practice. Freedom is the basis, even stolen freedom or, which is no longer yours, there are many hidden concepts that you don't say, you don't speak is what? they make repentant theories pass for degradation or, freedom no longer yours, too many films about extortion in general. Now one passes by and takes you away. Immoralities surpassed in good, malicious words or software that have necessarily been eliminated, to live without fear and degradation.

It exists somewhere else but, an evil may come here too, it presupposes a living past, a spiral of souls passed into life. It was necessary to make some things clear, now it's too late, but as never before, things like problems are the same in time, one day it will be solved if there is a subject, the problem is always that one, then a whole is formed and it's always them, then things are done and, it's always those.

Environments, figurative structures and imprisoned in the eyes of all, one day they will come to light, you will learn the changes, you say it's all over, what you earn today. Look at people or, what they do, what they wanted to do, you'll believe that it's longer the road, it's many things still to begin, for this and other reasons. The person is not just my business or, yours as you say. In the existence of a body or a function is the same, you live and it is a general matter, one is here, then it will be somewhere else. Take the right line, because it is not forbidden to go one way instead of the other, true or not you can go in all directions freely but, you can see from here that they are all very awkward, as usual with that question of an evil, and then they left it there, and it is always the same in time.

The existence is a charming game, the only thing that remains without doubt present and true. Deceptive sometimes, however, you've fallen in love with doubt, they say that it does not resolve, it will remain over the years, this is the way you want to tell you, your happiness, relaxation you know, there is nothing better, peace then I explain, please. Where are you going to run off to again, Mrs. Bene whatever your name is, this way you won't even go anywhere. You'll be great and you'll see behind you that certain situation that hasn't been solved, it may belong to others, but it will be virtue to appear. Those objective realities that no one wants to declare will be said all, the gardens and what remains. It's starting now, but we need everything else, as we'll see later. I'm on vacation is like a game, don't ask the work to last forever, it ends and it's a complete fact, it was what you had to do. What others will do, instincts to infection, extinct instincts. Eliminate the human being's ability not to progress, whoever you want is interested in power games in August, now it's all solved. They are thieves, but those who steal remain fooled, it is always so the joke ends up that you cannot say, whoever made a mistake does not accept the law of the state, what is illegal lives as a parasite over ideas. This holiday seems like oil, a life always wants its measure, what do you want next September without love, without a denunciation of what you could do or be, but it will be the business of others, as those who have said now is no longer possible. Here we are all already gone, one is better off without the problems of others, the rat that makes us accept nothing, an evil is an absurd, an emptiness.

Appearances are the main kindnesses, everything ends here is nothing you can do, we are small at the bottom and we will remain firm. Who has stolen now wants him to own what he has taken, as if he had bought it, there is a story in life that says that is not the train that comes to pick you up, it is instead so that you renew an evil not to believe, choose God or the State and it is better that you continue, people are not perfectly informed, sometimes who knows who, time informs them is a realm of photocopies. Existence always needs to be refreshed, we live among false people of no small importance. There is an order even two or three, you are in operation if you are alive, who is alive is registered. Nothing ends everything is transformed, nothing changes there, nothing changes there, everything is defined as firm in its position, as you want to change a state in place, words must stop to bring in silence, you must not speak, they are past programs, serious not yet resolved, they will end in acts of denunciation in the future, we will always be done with that story for a long time, while they have yet to find the new good, they are finished is locked in a cage, if you can escape if they show you a way believe it, if they give you the right indication. The word does not cancel itself is part of those personal things, which continue in other people, then it comes back to us, people believe that 'evil has won, people who will not live today.

I'm on vacation too and I think I'm on vacation everything is solved sea, sun, fish and other beauties, come on you look if even in summer you find fifteen or sixteen problems, so to live better. A note when everything ends and is over, there you have to start all over again, so we know, so you will do what you think is impossible and will not happen again or, what instead you can also say that it is better to do. Bad stories of past times, where the past meets the present, is the future the same. A software makes us determine what is right and, where to go in the future, we study to find order, sometimes cleanliness. Big words don't believe, they don't have a military purpose, afterwards there would be no more to look beyond but, great ideas shatter in the eyes of our modern, social and bureaucratic. The will has changed is no longer what you see, they hurt us and you think of something else.

Ruin, ruin things that don't work... it's summer, it's solved. What don't you want to make people walk after a spring spent working? I'm not talking about internal systems, but if you die you don't live anymore, the world has changed, already in a possible access of evil to begin with, there could be new times of employment or responsibility. What remains is not true, we won't find who did it, we need to live according to new canons, we need an art form, not a movement to do this, we don't need what we are interested in anymore. There is a new world after that foul-smelling toxic cloud, it is no longer ours to look at but everyone's, the better the house would look and, the chores to be done. Many things today you will find done to forget, no need to buy boredom, quitting is a form of purchase. The provenance is a study already done, while it is already a serious mistake not having told you what you have to do, how and how bad it is. Social or vocal structurally have changed, the verse of the turn is to want someone or something. A hell is a plague or, it's not a true, you need to regain personality, by the way, even years more what they stole from us, do not believe that the people of this summer will not run away, but you certainly pay.

No observance of the law, commanders and subjects pinching each other, it all seems normal. Stop signs are included in our city, breaks are a must. Another year you'll see the changes, the things you can't erase, they've already changed but certain passages can't be denied, whoever commands will disappear, they won't build themselves a house. Ruin, ruin a big problem that comes from some remote time passes for the best solution, what do you think? What remains is what counts but, I repeat, it's a strange world, you always turn around to return to the same point. Those who say they've been caught, that they want to manifest their art, have never seen an exit! Don't tell me that an evil is erased and everything remains the same, unchanged. A trick leaves things unfolding on their own for a while and it's all understood. A good, an evil like other associations between these two possibilities, is on the side who increases the thought in certain things, not inflatable. You are the main interest in your story, it is the others who must have this interest. Sometimes it's better to remain silent, it's better to say something to go away.

A hand out from people, thousands of problems that no one has solved, what you have never had, the impossible that wants to become reality, the contagion, the infection, the worm, all hidden too much, things that you should not do anything about, if not run away for the future, the existence camouflaged what the hell kind of history is this, a cash register is enough, there are no people treated like that, there is a rule to stay standing, and do not die. It's better to talk about which side you start from, sometimes you get over a problem but not saying it doesn't exist, it's already been decided what weight people can carry, time clarifies it can take ten years but, on one side you enter and you go, more and more inside towards the end. Every speech is finished and reachable in its situation... as soon as you are, we will be. Dreams are real realities, living what you want to call the best. A dream is the basis of modern reality, not just those things that were discussed before, evil, good two chapters of history, literature, law that is also modern. And we're still here, aren't we? The problem is no longer a problem, if I hugged him close. Past history of being in the eighties but, since the twentieth century every question is already seen and known, a past history, a difficulty, a photo or a film, images of controversial serve not to be alone. Never again without it is my motto today or, of those who have looked ahead, there will be someone who has not yet seen the way home but, exists and knows it. If you get everything here, there is no end to life, death, salami or bread. You're only wrong not to say that there is an evil, once you understand what it is, how it exists, it doesn't exist. Money spent in ignorance will create certain public problems... now you can be free. To have a good is never to commit an evil, I'm sorry if they didn't tell you before, but it's a necessary turning point, like saying no forever, so that you don't have to answer to anyone anymore. No, under no circumstances should you slit your wrists, evil is where they want it. You'll see they are the image of a thief, it's us who want the money, the power, it's not to die.

An evil ends with an evil, the annulment of memory, the depersonalization of the ego, the burial of the living form, the denial of the law. This you will always find us, forever, I believe connected to the shoulders of people who erase normally, how do you do it? you look at what happened to others, not to end up like the others. Here it's all fake, short and liar but there's a good thing, really like Indiana Jones, see you soon a kiss. It's a quality he doesn't understand, he usually never understands, he doesn't stop while life adapts instead to what the day is, then you can use various tools at your disposal to do.

Bad things don't happen, it's the point where the interpretation stops, the solution is: if only who is true in the function of an evil, which is then a void or a thick blow on the head. Everyone has the plague, just as we are all on our way to the other side. They have erased your conscience and you don't know it... I tell you it will be a game for the rich or, after all, a party to vote for, for every occasion. They'll make it happen again after your own good, if that's the way it was in the rest of the world. Here it is forbidden to deny a past, money, wealth, good music, America, the usual toys. You study so as not to assume an evil, you don't know the problems that are around, what happened, what the others think. You tell them where you've ended up or, that you're not evil, they lynch you...

calm down, I didn't even want to tell them the gap between good and evil. Words disappear when it comes to other people's business, too much work for people. Summer is vacation, the rest will be jail and death. You want to talk again like a strange man, here nothing else has begun, nothing else and thieves of inventions for a living. At the end of the mountain is the term, it will seem strange to you but this game has already been done, all the things of these discussions have already been studied and understood. The institute is the institution, as many things are no longer part of us and, others we would like to guarantee prison. Clearly you do not solve a problem in person wanders, yes it is the location, a summer at the beach, then a legal institute makes sure that 'our question everyone knows, because the problems are not ours but everyone's, you cannot imagine what people do to get good, some do not speak from the beating or disappointment. What do you want me to tell you we are not alone you don't believe us but, now you are on holiday relaxed, for sure all the work has been done, here are all the solutions on this table.

Sometimes you fly just for the sake of remembering the past years, the speech that was the same, ditto, the same. Just leave your badge on the table before leaving, it's those things you didn't need to do at all, you always continue not doing those things, then you forget not to do them, not doing them is still from a distance you will see the fruits and the pleasure of not having done what he asked you, continue passively or actively never doing evil. you live to look at the rest, you and the other neighbours, far away. What you don't have to do, you don't say! it's totally forbidden then, freedom begins and you find people who have been cheated by death in life.

Nothing ever changes, free yourself from things to be true, do something else. Out of evil, out of life to scandal, I don't think the boys in the future will live and, they will enjoy these things, knowing is not knowing, being wrong is forever. Laws are the rules for the intestine, you can or you can't so as not to get hurt, what a trouble the often-modern life, there is no solution to that function. Live peacefully, no one can treat people like that and let them live, it doesn't work, to tell you who doesn't exist.

The assumption of refusal is a well-known thing, the law is purgatory. Having sex has always been a ruin, ruining is the speech, what others do. Realities that are part of a changed world, boundless by the normal use of being, even in habits and things to do, maybe it's a bit too difficult but, anyway, we will learn. It's always just evil you have to talk! better not talk, stay silent or, not be there at all. They are diseases what you want to swallow, after you are at your starting point, your life was part of this story, do not lose do not worry, when it happens you're dead or dead. This is us, this is our life that is envied and mistreated, but it is not lost, there are so many forces and measures to win again, if you are you and I am me, we will see each other again if fate wants it to be so, fate is you beyond. Where are you going today? It's an exaggeration to think.

Silence is golden, an act, a perceptive sense of presence. After a good breakfast, there is nothing better than smoking, the holidays are spent to say serene, the girls run, they leave and then come back full of commitments. And you, and I, and who among us, would like but then legal matters, chores to do at home before going out. I think about the months of future work, I think a lot of bad things are already over because it wasn't me, because it was you. When the poetry is over, yours and mine. The relationship between two people, of non-summer business, we'll talk about it in September. Ten days after the holidays, the truce and peace. Victory is near, where are we going to end up? the speech lights up, we're in a sea like fish.

To the realities there is an end not concrete, they will be transported to another environment. Realities that have changed, something has happened, one does not live normally as they say, one does not live to solve problems forever. Do you have ruined beliefs? Already from the beginning is what had to be is where, peace on flowers and words is still flowers and blackberries, the mountains in a summer, as big as a dream.

Bye, G.

14.
An ash ceiling

15.09.2008

September where it is, the mystery of history begins again, what to do, is where. It's better to go so as not to get lost. Even this is forbidden to think, what is negative or a wrong accent, in a fold that didn't go well at all. We already lost today, the fourth day of the month! It'll be the air, what we wouldn't have done, and other lightness, ignorance, the weight of others. Thieves, murderers, the heaviness of the day... of what we must do. Where's that pencil gone? New things, rules to be put in place, things and houses.

Once October arrives, everything will be regular, only fear is nothing roasted or, one cannot say that impotence stops us, who knows how far we enter a dead habitat. Only you are still here, me and other solutions, it would be necessary to operate to let out an evil, it is again inserted into the body on one side, again it still seems past, instead there is no one. A past history jumps into the present, what do you want to find strange? If you don't bury the past properly, around here all it does is stand out in your face or, somewhere in your body... what a nice cut you have just to use. Well, thank you. It's certainly not your fault, but what you're arguing about, it's either the other's fault or an unresolved evil. It's us, but no he takes all the time or the company, don't you think he's got you, alone he doesn't get you, it's the society in constant change.

The laws are the trusted rules, always in the same daily stories, the repetition that repeats us, the past years oppress us to create a present full of problems, today disappears, and the problems come ahead. Everything is present also something more, that should not be there, you should not complain here or there, but towards the center.

Alone or in company you are the main person of existence, you compress the space closest to you, it is for others. Ignorance is the worst of illnesses, but if you talk to an evil the solution does not exist, fascism is serious, the return recovers us, there is no need to use a static form, continue and you only do yourself well. A public lawsuit, a complaint, the prison for those people is the dream or, the main nightmare of the day, which continues for October. Only the emptiness, all the emptiness is ignorance that must be defeated, it seems to you that one gets big then endures, do as I do in squares or, in lines, leave that place, which does not exist, where Italy grows and should live.

Division between parts and objects, you study mathematics serves in everyday life, some say it can not be applied to the nature of man, will have much to do today. A new day begins tomorrow too, if you don't organize something in this world nobody will do anything to you. What's better to avoid, ignore what you've already lost or, you don't even understand, wait until he wakes up to take him somewhere else. Trust me, trust is such an important thing. Adults keep some intellectual content for themselves, to live and see better, as a way to settle down.

Flying is like love, but it's mathematics, laws that not here but, in many places in this country are forbidden just to think about them, today as tomorrow but, not forever, nothing lasts forever. Evil never wins, it's a study just to stay or, it's just acts of illegality, slander, robbery in many ways and removal of self. Who wins this morning is what we have left, it's Sunday things go on as normal, but not as usual. What has to come, comes. A stormy sea, closed. Life is varied for how many people there are, we are the law and all creation. Here comes the coffee, good day.

Just pictures of diseases, things you don't say. Silence, things not liked and surprises, of a very different world, from what is said to be, on the obvious and normal side we do not continue, it is not made for others but for ourselves, after all what remains is the void, what is not accepted, afterwards will come our space. Reality is a concrete realization of everything and everyone, of what is around us, a complex of ideas that in the end make light concrete, who does not know for everyone is like that, alone or in society you can not fall back, to be is to become. Turn on, sit down and watch the spectacle that life gives you back, for what remains, to young people to grow up.

Constructions on constructions, things that are not needed, photocopies of life, false images, idolatries. Good anti-rule rules... stay still because the world is moving, that thing still exists there, where it will end! where a river ends. Objects and memories that didn't need to be added to everyday life, because of whom, the fault is already one, it's evening I'm not very hungry, I smoke another cigarette then I decide. Staring is very important in certain moments like these, there is the possibility of being already born, someone one day will save us, certainly things are not as they say.

Creation is an act of birth, you are like that because you were born or born like that, not just anyone made you, somehow you are like that now. They're not invited, do you want to find out who they are? The world has never stopped for a moment, even our parents are the way they are, people, life. You're the one who has to come forward on your own for your correct path, too much effort would be better a cooperative, a tool to have a less heavy job for everyone, you say it would be better to think about something else now it's evening, too much effort. It's a day like any other, who tells you not to believe in anything, instead insists on another full-bodied reality, with many ideals, mathematical reasons, solutions, depends on who you attend. Reality is not an easy thing, linear without any hope but, a creation, takes place in many different ways, and is projected into the future that is certainly happy. The concreteness of all the mathematical and legal ideas, you get back the account of the sentences and the houses in place as they were before, even afterwards, but in the meantime this is where the uncertainty takes place, where the problems should not be. People do not know what to invent in order to stay, while forms of thought, of words propose to form a new day, a current future from today already, you could not throw all those things or thoughts because they were not so good. American diversity, they are not the infinite limits where to go to parry. Unconscious and persistence where one goes to live, what was below did not exist, and it is already all somewhere else.

Fused thoughts, non-concrete realities that we live today, ignorance, ignorance, lack of knowledge, ignorance, oblivion of memory, you can't run away, you have to make yourself capable, he said it's all false, he denied the existence of that good that you bring for me, and it's true is who makes horror from that even all those evils // // for those who instead live beyond it has always been a dream but, really, it's only for a few. Here we are not where we were said to be, there is no world of equalizing what you want, there are, you are, they are not, and it's all true. Quality is to be yourself always, more deeply, in any part and place. Things and houses, colours but fantasy is sympathy. Today's topics at lunch, tango and stones. People do not speak for fear of making a bad impression, that indecency stops itself, like buying a new rolling pin, real Italian, what do you want me to say, have a good appetite.

Unsurpassable people, unmatched are the most wrong people on Earth, nobody speaks even in a close relationship nothing comes out of it. Look, they are your enemy, your best friend, excuse my air of mockery but the experiences are like at school, how you go out or finish studying, always not getting hurt possibly. How sharp is the air of success in God you understand where you are, those bad words do not say them, the beginning is which way, how to light a match.

The hourglass of time plus what you are not, speeches that are made during the day, things that are not repeated, things that are not said or cannot be said, things that are known and taken away, forgotten, stolen, sometimes so wrong that they even make mistakes, it is not even necessary to know where they light us or access us, a common speech is not looked at, you do not want to attack those who must, for what the duty given to him, here the absence is normally.

Our whatever, sometimes one has to be a singularity to be so, the world has departed. They went out and never came back, the other, the others, the big ben are only one thing, the world has changed. Peculiarities in unequal spheres, events have changed for us too. Positions of our ideas, constructions of history in the day and time, the motor arts, for a long time what we do not accept is reality, who wants to complain about the powers or, who has nothing to do with it. We are not what is invented but, what we are inside that you can lean on, and then solve and build, I would like to know how that story ended! Rest, rest, what it must be is. Who's lost but, what the hell kind of talk is that. No, it's all wrong an evil, outdated, if you can get there you'll find some fresh air. It works like you said before you speak, it's just mountains of rubbish, go with your shovel and work it out. When you don't want those cursed attributes, yours, mine, or you don't want those lucky realities not to end, they are options that few people feel for themselves, it's not the air but our suffering, our indifference that they create today.

The world has changed I don't understand, what shouldn't it be, the rest doesn't matter? Good is light for a few, others must suffer, false fascists. Art is useless, no! If anything, it's the road you can't see, because normality is an evil. The future solves problems, even those with fascism. The future is after, tomorrow, a year from now, you can't pay so much attention to what you thought or did in the past, what has been done is always a mistake, isn't it? The truth already resides in us but it must always be cleaned, washed day by day, so the idiocy disappears for our tomorrow, so we will see another world growing.

Countless faces, faces, vaults and turns of the same game to say what you should not know, always that refrain, where we bend is nothing else, that dissolve and destroy, there is no explanation. A cylinder, a cone is what you are. Another virtue is needed, here is the cut, or the law of the cursed cut.

There was nothing better than another coffee... it's international what is ours, have a good weekend.

A hug G.

15.
It is a shocking identity crisis

30.09.2008

"What I want to say to you is a daily question, a search where not to lose but, to find the being you, the being me. Certain things that are true every day, you study mathematics, computer science, religion, love. From where one hunts the void, the roof is beyond the void, the others arrive by observing the objects."

My theory is an open, spontaneous, clear statement about the objective realities present. On Sunday morning, October 5, two thousand and eight are in a hotel in Rome, in the centre of Aurelia antica street, it already seems as if memories of a time that has passed, of a civilization that has worked. When I come back I'll tell you about the people who made mistakes, there is no going back, there are many reasons, you don't play with things or people you don't know. The depth before the surface, it seems easy, then it is not a way to offend, it is not bad. We return crazy well, we and people who do not know, then betrayed, fail. Grows an evil, otherwise we are mistreated at the bottom, but where there is nothing more, you cannot know what is the bottom, does not end up only in a cruel solution. There's no going back, it's not true that we won't do anything anymore, we'll do it later.

Wish me good day and, a carefree return, how many things there are still to do. Title, it seems night instead it's real dark, after all I have to do something else, what don't you know, why aren't you here? Already true is all false but, it's true everything even where you stopped, the real point where you're standing still, where there is no more me or anything else, they did us in the past, even a good thing. Emptiness hurts, what used to hurt us remains, afterwards it will hurt, it doesn't erase everything in this city, it seems but it's not true, what remains is us that is nothing but, everything you can imagine. Maybe you're thinking about what you could say, about what nobody here has done, nobody tells us or does, but normality explains everything to those afterwards.

What it had to be is, what you have to do if you don't know, if you go a bit further. Nothing you can do for those usual problems, because now you are tired, what do you want to find in a brick if not freedom, look that you do not fall down there, without an explanation, outside are just images of the return home, or a memory full of people telling you, you have to expand your thinking and other places at the same time that create your own. They were gags not to understand, going back means in those places or ideas where the evil things were, where you can only understand, the world was of those who will be later, who will be, it's never who they showed up tonight, for without you see it. You feel that it wasn't like that, it's others you're a part of but you're not there. Take a break no one is offended, here there's too much time, the usual moments are not enough to see but what remains. Nothing better than a cold fizzy drink, that day when they were calm and, without end, memories. The time that passes means a path, better not say, it doesn't pass anymore, it's like going to the doors without a permit.

I love Rome, it's like a lullaby that makes children sleep, you meet many old people and even much older buildings. The word begins already, it would be easy to get free, without even a gun. To be renewed of being or of others, that I am or I am not, where has the project gone: you are upstairs Rome or, it is better to look then, that the palaces are not yours, the ruins are eaten by men. A modern being where it goes to parry, without what you know, in the normality there are problems, there are associations, freedom of speech, you have to write the rest of the sentence, I do not want to talk anymore, you want a coffee is a necessity of belonging, otherwise how to say you know or, you are not there. They killed the evils there, didn't they? Conceptually it's just getting out of the speech, a personal alienation not to believe in a fake, there are thieves of ideas and thoughts like those of any other object. Once you get over what nobody says, you make it up: you prefer to talk to the present. The truth is in a police station, you have to solve problems with time, then something else like children and salary.

A continuous duplication of our being is an ignoramus who doesn't want to disappear, a delinquent who pretends. Problems that mortify everyone, they are not theirs, they don't belong to them, if you talk to someone about them they say that nothing could be done, not even knowing who they are going to start talking to. Palaces, colours, plants, florists and I am also in this as they call the sea, but in reality it must be the common. You know sometimes it's better to continue at another time, somewhere else. Obvious places unknown, because there are those who say there is wrong then, you do not know who you're talking to, it's a crisis of blindness only this. Problems are limits or, there are people who are problems, the world is wrong where we are, the images to turn to are false, not awake but, things change sometimes forever, it's the fear of another evil. In Rome there will be the State, where to go not to get lost, it is a dream to be in this city. I will be there is not a way to say but, for starters already, we do not talk about it, now the problems are in line like others intermittently or, the light has gone out. A continuous backward progress friend, a continuous making of stuff, accessories but, careful understanding is not part of the moment, just continue with these damn feet, who have done wrong are sinners, in too many things you do not say anything. True is in the air, it's already over. What happened is not known, who will speak is the non-participant. Only mathematical calculations before going to sleep, nobody lives together with whoever they want, instead it's a whole other side of what could happen. Without God or with your back turned you want to know then, if you are not present where the law applies more than anywhere else, there are many things you cannot say, the other year he stops where he says he arrived, there is nothing on that side, there resides death life, then it seems the same thing that contract, speech.

Remember, you smell the usual story arrives, autumn anticipates winter, the reverse. Calm is rest, perfumes that know about the same question but, of what year who knows! I would pay to have peace but, maybe you don't buy it, what problem is what you remember, it is always better not to talk but, if there is no one, just moved or lost, is how many social problems if you look at one side. One that you laugh at has a plastic face and, an endless ear of corn, then we'll see to make it disappear, how we are, what we were supposed to be, what they'll tell us to do, there won't be a solution, nobody wants it. Absolute peace comes in winter, even if with a few little thorns... like a nothing closed tomorrow, we'll live better, we'll see each other again if we don't die. You've never heard of total deficiency, you've never heard of it or, remember you've heard of it. The world comes down from here then, it is the construction for freedom, it is always a solution does not come, it is not found but it is not true, that it does not exist. Where there is no higher one arrives, where there is no more than saying, there remains the guilt of the evil inserted in our society, therefore in our software, thought, action or act. As long as it lives where it remains, the unhealthy is not ours, but complaining is the least one can do, tradition is culture, that is, we are not lost forever. It would be better to use a telephone, smoke a cigarette... the memories of a past day, the time that passes is the memory that is lost without trace.

Flying higher to go where you've never been, those damn clichés. What you could never do is where the sentence ends, where those things we no longer have, boxes that should contain us in darkness and, in blindness, it is forbidden to grow up and know them, something that bothers us too much, too much at times. Worthless words are no use where we will go tomorrow, it is already better what we did not do today, without respite possible future, are attacked not to live, not to exist is the solution! Business as grown-ups who move so far away the voice, we need an application of arguing but, without that dilemma or gain. Fear of being mocked or dodged, issues of the past but if you want are just objectivity to discuss openly, even today better in a public office, to see what they will do tomorrow, who goes to work in a public office. Among other things, talking is like continuing, it seems to shoot without uncertainty, against people harmless on the surface. Heaven and emptiness then a means of work, tomorrow it will be a war, nobody says it to themselves or to a colleague, tomorrow we have already lost everything, continue as if there would still be ... we have said almost nothing, a few glances, we said goodbye, tomorrow the Sun comes out hopefully then, down to the end of the existing technique without jamming. I know you're anchoring for the night at your place, almost everything is forbidden, except the catastrophic false fascism.

It seems to you that I'm wrong to move this damn pen, but they are things that we have around us, you have to write them down, it's night seems late, where do you want to end up if not in bed, it was all that night, where I remember you weren't there, how can we do it, you don't have to know, how badly it exists here or there, just this one sentence, that you could know. Enter where you could denounce me, death ends where you realize that you are alive, you are not yet sleepy, or you are another, another.

That day away, without knowing where you weren't, the day you died, is very fashionable lately. It's not all false, otherwise what's true is what's true, or hunger, or colour. Okay, in five minutes

Dante but even more down, you know what I'm talking about, without taking away tomorrow's work or, the obvious, the time, where the hell we were shot, that is the false already, it must be time to wash up to go to bed. Sleep, sleep, still sleep, that double-tongue is a disease, you know what doesn't exist, to do is the last meal of what was there and, there won't be any more, tell me what's going on or, the difficult things it's better not to do, how many nonsense there are hidden, the time that advances is not a bad thing, you need to open your eyes right where we are, to see what we really have then, it's all in order, Dad. Whoever says it will all be erased, the subject is included in the things we have done and, in the things we can't do, there's no need, who will ever be there after the door? many people have come to tell us again to confuse us... and everything is lost in life. If I really knew it was someone else, I'd better not tell you who it would be or, better I'd tell you, pause. So you're not me, I'm not the lawsuit is a requirement. We don't have personalities that aren't our own, we don't want to fight about things, we live what's around us and, part of us.

The video is very spicy as business, what we do, the organisms that we are not, because they have emptied us, I could go on for a long time but, I have a strange desire to get paid. Sometimes you know is the useless, so I stop because there is a ban, yes the rest is in a full parking lot, we get lost as we lose the place, and we have to find a new one. People who point out, there's no such thing as I don't know, who knows, who knows. I already have the ammunition and the picture of what it was supposed to be, it's not true we will disintegrate. Old stories like models who want to finish or, stomachs in the streets, age, the taste of perdition, the falsehood of an acquired disease or, the disregard of what is already lost. I lost, who lost? I keep walking so much you don't know, you know how many people say to please tell them, it's nobody who knows. Habits or ways of everyone to be revealed to stay afloat, without blows and other things then, who wants us ignorant to govern us. Nice words, toys. We'll still be on time.

I've finished. Bye, G.

16.
Double freedom

30.10.2008

"Good morning, you know sometimes it's really difficult
A monument, an ancient public work of our city."

Listen well, there's still an evil already, he's about to do another round-days then he won't solve it, you'll be appalled. There's no better way, go away because they are. All this was not wrong but, a form to recognize themselves, where it ends is where you're going, what you want to do to us is the fruit of a society, where evil lives. His half is down in hell, what he doesn't know or, can't explain. It seems easy but winter, the inverse arrives, you have to take off that cap, which does not make you feel to know more, today as you go somewhere else. Or free double freedom, the West in a single word, to make others talk you find what you didn't have to do, as yesterday evening passed, of course you can see the East is to think that you are in Italy. State or death the differences in business, losses and crimes because here we still discuss who goes and who does not go. A repetition is what we would have done wrong, nobody wants to do anything, there is an evil as a specialty of thieves. Dissolutions of being so no one arrives, where you have already gone, where you want to go, the law is already, entrust it to her does not betray, you will not get lost for everything. What is written is clear, it does not lie then people are or are not, you always live a little lower than what we are, and it is our fault. Hermeticity is our time, which one will go to today.

It appears this way, the denial of what we were saying, to find ourselves in a wrong form, is to accept to be an imprecise, after we continue to recover. It works for all the things we want, and it is in all things, our life always because we know it, there are plans on it also because its entire duration is not always. Knowing where we are going, what we are going to do, where we are going to move is not an offense, the bad things, the insults, we must always look for them in evil, so you find yourself.

There'll be nothing left here but whoever tells you, the spirit is the flesh. A software, for example, where we're going, is already solved without problems. I'm feeling a bit pulled, he must be the monster of the municipality or, what he wants to achieve, he thinks he doesn't even know what he wants, where he will be wrong is when we will win. After that it's all brands, sub-brands of various products, if we get there poor Italians, what do you want to happen only the end? after all this what can you expect, after an evil, a good then only life. What is that norm to work and die, what can you see, close your eyes and go on, there is the door. Good doesn't anyone say that? Isn't it forbidden? We're still in evil, it's still got to happen. You find someone to explain it to you, it's again we go where we didn't want to go before, so it works until it ends badly, for a while then the rest is the air we breathe, it's what we have left to live, while we are still there we have to leave, we don't know why.

Rules of traditions that we want to take away first, instead enter our flesh to betray and hit, where we do not know that we are not another. Reason is population, memory is the limit as we do not know where to stop is who to call, who are these people who even now are here to annoy us. Now it's still, go on with your day, you've always done it. You will see people then there are other things, which are not immorality, because you know what you were doing today, afterwards only God has thought about it, who knows the state of people.

Everything is bad, so many insults however you go on, maybe there is someone there to talk to us. Now there's nobody left, you know the song of how life goes on, always at the starting point, every intention seems vain, you know nobody ever says anything. Invent him the place where to live, for them every ending is wrong, every beginning is a dead end, who says that absurd instead is only the starting point or that it is necessary to do it alone leave it alone, a common questionnaire is not a personal business, you will never stay alone already, how many doubts where there is a point, while the radio continues to play, you have never started a project to always execute the good thoughts but think about the good, is not only solve that damn questionnaire, if you are in Europe at the home of those who have wrong the future, given also to no one, we will only find ourselves at the home of those who are right or, of those who are wrong, not in that magnificent paradise, where you talk freely and, the problems solved already, you continue if the tension increases, a good coffee brightens the memory of time, now is the reality of all time. I have just returned from a trip near here, where I don't go every day because of constant work commitments, everything seems immaculate, just the crisis of the almost neighbour and not believing in our expectations, the mind where it empties, we continue in a circuit that leads to the end, the loss of belief in truth, the replacement of teeth, the deficiency. Here, on the other hand, there were impulses. What you can't do, don't do, isn't yours. Protect yourself, as in Mass, go along the most upright path without thorns, I beg you not to call, it hurts the part of your face where he says you are not there, you will do it. The solution to every question exists, you believe in it so go to the street where he says it is there, better than there is, nobody has ever touched it, afterwards you will find what you want of it, that it doesn't exist. Peace be that together but, there is a dark cloud over the city, made of evil demons, what questions you ask we'll see later, if there is time to go.

All that is needed is marked, recorded for you or for me also, what in the years to come from these precipices, which prepare the dinner and afterwards. Mark everything, record as you see, the State is still missing if not for the daily novels magazines, it must always be recorded all life, to have a complete vision of the day in a universal way, I believe in one God but, still after all we do not know, the difference is necessary. The ignorant take advantage of our ignorance, disharmonious objective materiality, what you think since yesterday we were not together. Never forget an evil, it is written on the door of the house, my head tells me other things, more than what we expected for today, cleanliness, the risk of where to go, the dream is not hallucination but true, the act we must do today organized. Happenings happen by themselves, the dream continues the day together but, unfortunately, it has false, false idols. The day is without idiocies for which, it couldn't be better or worse, the air makes new changes, new shades that improve the quality of life, there are laws that have never been used or censored and, laws used in a wrong way.

Living on the road, tell me all about life and progress that have betrayed us, what made us wrong, what you had to say or do, of roads that we have never travelled, then tell me the worst stuff is he / she. Progress is not a bad story but a matter of millions of Italians, instead of what a strange day it was today, I met people but, not as usual, then that normal wall, it seems to be in Berlin not in Cosenza. Usual things, holes in the abstract streets to go home, now I feel safe normal no! A conspiracy against the earth or life, it's not the good, what you thought you couldn't say, it was what you had around you, the immoral instead of what it was supposed to be, the most beautiful flower of our life, it's you know how many misfortunes even before arriving, where peace is life. It's the fault of unspoken realities and, of things that are also people, ideas are already bodies, rubble. Ideas are the best fruit, an idea is the solution then, people do not touch each other, they ruin themselves as realities are the law, you pay ask if there is someone, who shoots in the air there.

The future has escaped, you know, the future is gone, laugh, what you didn't know is happening to us, what's worse? I'm already here, I am my future. I have to see in the archive but, it seems there is nothing left, you know there is a ground floor where the earth, is more indicative of yourself, there you don't have to go and see, better is to find someone, something. We need peace in our Antichrist, it is said I have already had, avoid in the majority of an evil, we must recognize what was good and evil. Campanelle, at that time that was all they told us to do or, that we wanted, they wanted, and that's the whole way down from the floor of the house to the street, then we are in the memory.

What doesn't exist in this world is like ignorance or, as we all went to sleep while the problem, the famous question, even our own, was not yet solved. There are few people left, you always have to hurry, what you don't know is what you can't do. Do I smoke a cigarette or is it forbidden? I haven't read it somewhere. Nobody's talking here, it must be another problem, what we have on our side to understand each other or, what we won't have. Stay still is worse, let's separate presentations. They thought the human was a box then, he threw himself in the garbage at a certain age, instead it was us, it was us. Now, all we have to do is look around the room, dear real acquaintance. You even have to take care, and be good at throwing boxes away, sometimes some can be useful but, verbs are adverbs, here you go up or down for different ideas, all personal plans. Now, as usual, it's time to rest, I don't want to be rhetorical but, there is necessarily a need.

Just to tell her certain words are reality, instead of just fantasy, as thinking about her certain things hurt, but sometimes thinking is much better than acting, in five or ten minutes a day. It's called a project, you can say what you want, the result is its product, the road to achieve is always that, after the light of our great state industry, I've never heard of immune deficiency acquired, immune equals exempt but, how not to be aware of being sick or super, by the way then as it is after all, the rest of our lives, what we will not have lived, because we were at work, or engaged.

The expected winter has arrived, our clarity of mind is confirmed only if we talk about it. The laws of the state go fast, even inventions. No, don't leave it is what people need, it is unresolved problems that come back to solve them, or, not quiet people who could not solve them. What you want to ignore if you live in the bottom, even being a millionaire, the good is not a dead form, from which to draw to continue, to go forward. The good is us, we stop because we are mortal, everyone is mortal except God.

Words are used on the one hand not to be heard or in front of you to say them, if you need explanations ask her always, forever. Today at the end of November of the year zero eight, there are resolutions to ask for, as many as a mountain and, the usual false ones will only have to step aside, there is neither for them, only good for that exponential positive line. Reality is hidden but in truth it forms the possible and the impossible, life and death.

Living in the good is the same as saying tomorrow I'll go shopping but, nobody exists, nobody believes it, instead it's all possible existing! So even if we go out without lawyers, it would be the same. Impossible is nothing, it's millions of calculations. The trick is in the words, you have to repeat them backwards too, to find what you were looking for.

Bye, G.

Notes:

1. They live in evil, one like never, two like they hope. Luckier people do not exist, poison is born, then I am dead, I suffer because I live together with other dead people. There is a way to get where I imagine, if there is a way to go, we have to do it again, we are the ones who are here now in this time, maybe it was us also in the past centuries. We don't talk about normal things, if not for inner peace, we colour life, we make it exist. If you move, someone else shoots you, a cause causes an effect, it happens what it wants is good for one aspect, for others it doesn't.

2. I am still to learn how to use it without instructions. Originals are not spoken of in this place, only resemblances who knows what taste there is, to live without originals, you know some originals, will perhaps payments made or, what we would have in the eyes. The minutes that I have to wait here are few, that question is eternal as a life but, we have always done it.

3. Crush an uuencoded, unidentified noise, many times I see everything. The brain was something else than an immense expanse of flowers or cities, do you happen to lose all your teeth? Zero problems today, I think life is long, it's always time to learn, as long as time exists sometimes disappears, even other things or, people, by force you do not get anything good, convenient and usable. The good is another matter, as if leaning in the opposite direction cancels the success, you need to learn the good because it will serve or, in order not to always take a beating.

4. The subconscious not to move it in time is a public chamber, there is the possibility that it will be stolen or ruined, it is always necessary to recognize all the good to enter, from that to begin the day, not to talk about that topic, the disgust is not necessary.

5. The end, life is music that possibly must be able to play without any dissonance, you play an instrument without making mistakes or, a note throughout the piece. The smell of a cigarette without anxiety, the impossible things do not exist but, only other much more expensive, to leave sometimes. Those hunters, the world is a chair to sit and wait for the arrival. Actually I'm more of a painter than a writer, we still feel hello *G.*

"I conclude this second diary of mine, I think it could be interesting and useful for those who want to explore an emotionally true universe, a memory about a not far past that could be the world in today's events. I wish you the best for all the surprises that life has in store for you.
Good luck!"

Gerardo D'Orrico
https://www.beneinst.it

Index of contents

Index of contents

AN ASH CEILING

by Gerardo D'Orrico

English translation

by Fatima Immacolata Pretta

Publishing house TEKTIME

ISBN 9788835410997

www.ingramcontent.com/pod-product-compliance
Lightning Source LLC
LaVergne TN
LVHW020332200726
843507LV00012B/2330